PRAYING THE LORD'S PRAYER FOR SPIRITUAL BREAKTHROUGH

PRAYING THE LORD'S PRAYER FOR SPIRITUAL BREAKTHROUGH

ELMER L. TOWNS

This Billy Graham Evangelistic Association
special edition is published with permission
from Regal Books.

Regal

A Division of Gospel Light
Ventura, California, U.S.A.

Published by Regal Books
A Division of Gospel Light
Ventura, California, U.S.A.
Printed in U.S.A.

Regal Books is a ministry of Gospel Light, an evangelical Christian publisher dedicated to serving the local church. We believe God's vision for Gospel Light is to provide church leaders with biblical, user-friendly materials that will help them evangelize, disciple and minister to children, youth and families.

It is our prayer that this Regal book will help you discover biblical truth for your own life and help you meet the needs of others. May God richly bless you.

For a free catalog of resources from Regal Books/Gospel Light please contact your Christian supplier or call 1-800-4-GOSPEL.

Cover Design by Barbara LeVan Fisher
Interior Design by Britt Rocchio
Edited by Ron Durham and Virginia Woodard

Library of Congress Cataloging-in-Publication Data
Towns, Elmer L.
Praying the Lord's Prayer for spiritual breakthrough / Elmer L. Towns.
p. cm.
ISBN 0-913367-13-3
1. Lord's prayer—Devotional literature. I. Title.
BV230.T65 1997
226.9'606—dc21

Rights for publishing this book in other languages are contracted by Gospel Literature International (GLINT). GLINT also provides technical help for the adaptation, translation and publishing of Bible study resources and books in scores of languages worldwide. For further information, contact GLINT, P.O. Box 4060, Ontario, CA 91761-1003, U.S.A., or the publisher.

IN APPRECIATION

To Pastor Lawrence Williams, my childhood Presbyterian
pastor who told us each week, "Let us stand
and pray as our Lord commanded...."
Thank you for giving me a love for the Lord's Prayer.

To the public school teachers of Waters Avenue School in
Savannah, Georgia, who daily ask all pupils, Jews, Catholics
and Protestant, "Let us say the Lord's Prayer...."
Thank you for giving me a rich heritage.

To Yonggi Cho, pastor of more than 750,000 people in
the world's largest church...
Thank you for teaching me to pray daily the Lord's Prayer.

To the Pastor's Bible Class at Thomas Road Baptist Church,
where I taught the material in this book in seven
successive weeks...
Thank you for the opportunity of ministry.

To Linda Elliott, Susie Butler and Amy Sue Marston,
my secretaries...
Thank you for typing and editing the manuscript.

CONTENTS

FOREWORD

DR. YONGGI CHO

YOIDO FULL GOSPEL CHURCH
SEOUL, SOUTH KOREA
RECOGNIZED AS THE LARGEST CHURCH IN THE WORLD,
AND THE LARGEST CHURCH IN CHRISTIAN HISTORY

This book was born in a breakfast meeting with Dr. Towns several years ago. We are friends, and I had him speak to my people during our prayer meeting in 1978. Dr. Towns told me he wanted to be more godly and to have more power in prayer. At that breakfast meeting he asked me, "How would you advise me to be more effective in prayer?"

I told him, "Each day I pray the rounds. Like a runner who jogs around and around a race track to get physically fit, I pray the rounds several times each day."

Dr. Towns knows church history, so he knew what I meant. To pray the rounds daily is to pray the Lord's Prayer several times each day.

I believe when a person sincerely prays the Lord's Prayer each day, that person has covered the basic ways to worship God, and the basic ways to grow and protect his or her spiritual life. Like seed within fruit, the Lord's Prayer contains every requirement for which a Christian may pray each day.

I told Dr. Towns to pray the Lord's Prayer several times at the beginning of each day. Once is not enough. I told him to emphasize a different petition each time he prayed the Lord's Prayer.

When people pray the Lord's Prayer, they have covered every type of petition that will touch every aspect of their lives. That doesn't mean they have prayed for every need in their lives. It doesn't mean they have finished praying. After I pray the Lord's Prayer each day, I spend two hours a day in prayer touching many other requests.

Sometimes people must pray day and night. They have many requests, so they do not use the Lord's Prayer again and again. But the Lord's Prayer is a good place to start one's intercession. People pray all weekend at our Prayer Mountain and use the Lord's Prayer to begin their intercession. It is an important aspect of prayer.

When I say the Lord's Prayer touches every type of petition, I mean you will worship, ask for guidance, yield to God, ask for petitions, ask for forgiveness, seek victory over sin and end up in spiritual warfare in which you ask for protection from the evil one.

May multitudes read this book and begin daily to correctly pray the Lord's Prayer. If that happens, God's people will be revived and His church will do exploits.

Yours in the tender mercies of God,
Dr. Yonggi Cho
Seoul, South Korea

The Lord's Prayer

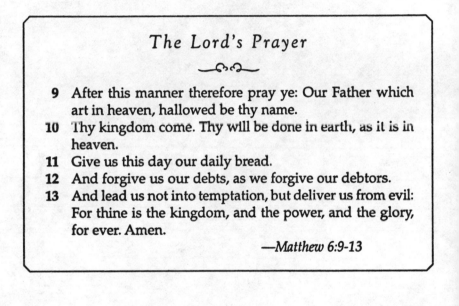

9 After this manner therefore pray ye: Our Father which art in heaven, hallowed be thy name.

10 Thy kingdom come. Thy will be done in earth, as it is in heaven.

11 Give us this day our daily bread.

12 And forgive us our debts, as we forgive our debtors.

13 And lead us not into temptation, but deliver us from evil: For thine is the kingdom, and the power, and the glory, for ever. Amen.

—*Matthew 6:9-13*

HOW I PRAY DAILY THE LORD'S PRAYER

My eyes pop open. From between the warm flannel sheets I peek at the digital alarm clock. The illuminated numbers tell me it is 5:55 A.M. My muscles ache because I got to bed late. Again, I did not get enough sleep. My body is half asleep, but my mind is already in gear. I begin thinking about all the things I have to do today.

I reach over and turn off the alarm. My clock is set for 6:00 o'clock each morning, but my mind is programmed to awaken a few minutes earlier.

I stretch under the sheets, then fold the covers to my waist. The rush of cool air on my chest awakens me. My mind and body are now on the same page. I am ready to start praying.

Even before I get out of bed I begin praying the Lord's Prayer. Some have told me they can't pray in bed. They claim they would go back to sleep if they did not get out of their warm beds. Once my eyes open, though, my mind starts percolating. I can't go back to sleep, so I am thinking even before I get out of bed. Instinctively, I begin to pray,

Our Father who art in heaven...may Your name be hallowed in my duties today...as Your name is hallowed in heaven.

Thy kingdom come...may you reign in my life on earth as You rule heaven.

Thy will be done...in my studying...teaching...counseling...as Your will is done perfectly in heaven.

Give me daily bread...for my physical strength...for all my needs this day.

Forgive me my sins...and the consequences of my sins ...including my actions and intent...and forgive others as you have forgiven me.

Lead me not into temptation...don't let sin overwhelm me, but give me victory today.

Deliver me from the evil one...protect me from physical and spiritual harm.

For thine is the kingdom...I recognize Your sovereign control of my life.

For thine is the power...I recognize Your ability to do these things.

For thine is the glory...I give You credit for every answer.

In Jesus' name...

Amen.

Before I get out of bed, I usually pray the Lord's Prayer. It takes about a minute. Now I am spiritually ready to begin my day. My main prayer time, however, is not while lying in bed, nor is it the main time I pray the Lord's Prayer. This is just my "waking up" prayer to get my day started right.

Some may criticize me for not going straight to my office for Bible study and prayer. If that is your pattern, please continue. Some of you may not have time for Bible study in the morning, so praying the Lord's Prayer in bed is better than not praying at all.

I turn the covers all the way back and slip on flannel sweatpants, then put on a flannel sweatshirt. A bathrobe is not warm enough for me. Going downstairs, I fix a pot of coffee—enough for me and my wife, Ruth. I take my vitamin pills, then jog out to the mailbox for the morning paper. Returning, I pour my coffee, (no sugar, but a little cream), and I turn on the TV to Headline News to get the overnight events of the world. In about 15 minutes I have finished my coffee, read the paper and I know what is happening in the world.

After I finish reading my paper and drinking my coffee, I am ready to go upstairs to awaken my wife. Before I do, I pour two cups of coffee, another cup for me to drink while I read my Bible, and a cup for my wife. I awaken her, put her coffee on the nightstand along with the morning paper. When my roses are blooming (the rosebush was given to my grandmother by my great grandfather in 1886), I bring my wife a yellow Carolina rose to brighten her day.

I then go to my office for my devotions with God. I do not have a set routine for my daily devotions. Sometimes I begin with prayer, usually starting with the Lord's Prayer. Sometimes I begin reading Scriptures—I try to read through the entire Bible each year. Sometimes I begin by opening my hymnbook to sing prayer hymns to God. It is easy to find prayer hymns—they end with the "Amen" refrain. Sometimes I begin digging into a single passage of Scripture for the Bible class I teach. Usually, though, I begin my daily devotions by praying the Lord's Prayer.

BRINGING GOD TO A HOLIDAY INN

One morning I woke up in a Holiday Inn. Holiday Inn rooms are drab olive green and gray...the same color scheme...the same room arrangement. A Holiday Inn room is not warm like my home. This particular day, the sun was hidden by a cloudy overcast. Moisture in the air gave it the scent of rain. Water dripped off the roof into a puddle outside my glass door. My muscles and joints ached because I had flown in late and had not had enough sleep. My coffee, breakfast and morning paper had not completely awakened me.

I did not feel as though God was in that Holiday Inn room. It felt as though He were a million miles away, and the overcast sky shut Him out. Forcing myself to read the Bible did not make me feel His presence or get my motor going. God seemed hidden from me. So I knelt by my Holiday Inn bed, looked to God in heaven and worshiped Him.

"Our Father who art in heaven...."

I paused to remember that He is an awesome God who has power to create the world...to run the world...but most importantly, I told God, "You are my Father who cares for me." I praised Him for his goodness. "God, You love me and look after me just as I take care of my family.

"Hallowed be your name...."

The word "hallowed" means "holy." So I prayed, "God be holy in my thoughts...be holy in my conversations...be holy in this day."

Next, I began singing the hymn "Holy, holy, holy! Lord God Almighty! Early in the morning our song shall rise to Thee."

As I praised God, I begin to feel His presence creep into the room like fog creeping over a city park. The otherwise drab Holiday Inn room began to brighten up. My outlook for the day warmed up. The weather outside was threatening, but I felt snug (you don't pray just to feel something, but feeling can be a by-product of prayer).

Praying the Lord's Prayer, I worship God. I am not praying about my concerns, but I am focusing on God. I have learned that when I worship God, He comes to receive my worship.

> When you worship God,
> He will come to you.

Jesus taught us that the Father seeks us to worship Him (see John 4:23). So when I worship God in obedience to the Bible, God visits a Holiday Inn room to receive the worship I am pouring out to Him.

Most people think God dwells in heaven. The Bible teaches, "The Lord dwells in the praises of His people" (Ps. 22:3—author's translation). Because God likes to be praised, He comes to hear what people are saying who are worshiping Him.

> If you praise God with your whole heart,
> He will visit you to receive the praises you give.

So God visited that drab Holiday Inn room on that drab day. His presence filled my morning and I felt Him. When I do not feel God, I worship him, and He comes to receive my worship. This all happens just because I begin my day praying the Lord's Prayer.

THE SEVEN PETITIONS

The Lord's Prayer contains seven petitions. The first petition is the worship of God..."*Hallowed be thy name.*" I have just told you that the presence of God comes when you correctly worship Him. In chapter 3, you will find several other benefits from making this petition.

When you pray the second petition, "*Thy kingdom come...,*" you are asking for help in living each day by Kingdom rules. You will find many other benefits in chapter 4.

Chapter 5 explains that God has a plan for your life, and if you will wholeheartedly pray "*Thy will be done...,*" He will help you find the best way to live.

The first three petitions are called the "Thy Petitions" because they center on God (i.e., *Thy* name be hallowed, *Thy* kingdom come, *Thy* will be done). To properly pray, you begin by focusing on God and His agenda.

The fourth is the "hinge petition" because it is attached to the "Thy Petitions." Just as a hinge is attached to a door that swings both ways, so this petition is attached to God's glory and a person's spirituality. The hinge petition is "*Give us this day our daily bread.*" "Bread" is a symbol word that denotes your physical life. You need physical life to glorify God and to live spiritually.

Once God gives you bread for your physical needs through the hinge petition, you are now ready to pray the final three petitions. These are called the "Us Petitions" (i.e., Lead *us* not into temptation, forgive *us* and deliver *us* from evil).

An overall view of the petitions in the Lord's Prayer looks like this:

"Thy" Petitions	**Praying for God's Glory**
"In heaven"	1. Thy name be hallowed,
	2. Thy kingdom come,
	3. Thy will be done.
Semi-conclusion:	*On earth as it is in heaven.*
The Hinge	4. Give us our daily bread.
"Us" Petitions	**Praying for Our Spirituality**
"On earth"	5. Forgive us our debts,
	6. Lead us not into temptation,
	7. Deliver us from the evil one.
Benediction:	*Thine is the kingdom, power, and all the glory.*

Each of these seven petitions contains many roots, just as the tree that reaches to heaven is supported by an unseen roots system that reaches into the ground. Many benefits are available to you as you pray each petition. Carefully studying this book will transform your life. You will walk closer to God; you will receive many answers to prayer.

I did not write this book to examine the meaning of each phrase of the Lord's Prayer...although you will gain some deep insights into the Lord's Prayer from this book. I wrote this book to help you talk to God...using the Lord's Prayer.

I did not write this book so you would memorize and repeat the Lord's Prayer mechanically each day, although I want to motivate you to pray it several times each day. I wrote this book so you would live and experience the Lord's Prayer.

I did not write this book as a tool to help you receive things from God, although properly praying the Lord's Prayer will help you experience answers from God.

I wrote this book to change your life.

A friend of mine is pastor of an Episcopal church and challenges his congregation every Sunday morning: "I know God...and this morning at this worship service, you can know God."

Then, standing in the clerical robes of his church, he offers the greatest challenge ever given a human audience that attempts to know God.

He says, "This week I have touched God, and this morning you can touch God. But more importantly, God can touch you."

I have written this book so that when you experience daily the Lord's Prayer, you can "touch God"; but more importantly so that right here and now..."God can touch you."

Sincerely yours in Christ,
Elmer L. Towns
Written at my home in the Blue Ridge Mountains, Virginia
Spring 1997

The Lord's Prayer for Me

My heavenly Father, may Your name be holy in me,
May Your kingdom rule my life,
May Your will control me,
May You be sovereign on earth as You are in heaven,
Give me daily bread for today's need,
Forgive my debts as I forgive my debtors,
Lead me not into temptation,
Protect me from the evil one,
Your kingdom rules in my life, Your power can do anything,
and Your glory is forever and ever,
 Amen.

~❧ I ❧~

BEFORE YOU PRAY:
HOW LONG IS ENOUGH?

Can You Pray for One Minute?

I stuffed myself into a tiny black closet. The walls and door squeezed in upon me, but I did not care. I knelt and faced the north corner. I was preparing for an unknown experience that was not dangerous, but I did not know what to expect, nor did I know what to do.

I was a 17-year-old college freshman, but being stuffed into a closet was not college hazing. I was not joining a fraternity, nor had anyone forced me into the closet.

The hardwood floor pained my knees. My bony knees were not used to one hour of kneeling. I was not being punished by the administration or a teacher. I had chosen to enter the closet of my free will, and I planned to kneel there for an hour...maybe two hours or more.

As a freshman at Columbia Bible College in Columbia, South Carolina, I enrolled in an introductory course about spirituality. The teacher had promised we would experience God before midterm exams. Because I was interested in spirituality, I wholeheartedly completed all the reading assignments. The one assignment I most looked forward to was praying for one hour. We were told to spend one hour alone with God in prayer. The instructor explained that we had to pray an hour because Jesus asked His disciples, "Could ye not watch with me one hour?" (Matt. 26:40).

Some of the students grumbled, and I have often wondered if they might have fudged on the time. Not me, though. Because I wanted to be spiritual, I meticulously prepared to pray for one hour. I set aside a Tuesday afternoon, from 2:00 to 3:00 P.M. because the dormitory was usually quiet during this time. My roommate usually was on the sports field, so he probably would not be in the room.

I had been assigned to room 427 in Legters Hall. Each room had tall ceilings and a fireplace. The hall had been built before the days of modern plumbing, but a glistening white sink hung on the wall in each entryway for casual washing. All plumbing and electrical wires were stretched visibly down the hall and along the walls. I called the dorm an elegant lady with a wrinkled face. The building was beautiful when she was constructed, but she had been born 120 years earlier. I offer this rather complete description of my dorm so you will realize it had only one tiny closet, one very small closet for me and my roommate's use. I squeezed into that closet because I read the words of Jesus: "When thou prayest, enter into thy closet" (Matt. 6:6).

Because I wanted to be spiritual, I took the command literally. Taking my coats and trousers off the hangers, I laid them on my bed. I did not remove my roommate's clothes, although I did remove his shoes, along with mine, and all the dirty socks. It is hard to put your mind on Christ when your nose is filled with foot odor.

The closet was only as deep as a coat hanger. I planned to kneel facing the north corner on my end of the closet. My feet would extend under my roommate's clothes. That is another reason I had to remove his shoes.

I planned to shut myself inside the closet for one hour because Jesus said, "When thou hast shut thy door, pray" (v. 6).

I prepared the closet 15 minutes early. My prayer requests were written in a notebook, so I rehearsed my list because I knew I could not see in the dark. Obviously, a beautiful old lady with a wrinkled face would not have a light in each closet. I placed the most important prayer request first on my list. If I had time, I planned to cover the less important requests in my second hour.

I did not pray nearly that long before going to bed at night. I had read stories of all-night prayer meetings, and I had heard about monks who prayed several hours each day. I knew I could not do that, but I wondered how long I could pray.

The college had printed a large-print "BUSY" sign on a cardboard for each room. When we hung out the "BUSY" sign, it meant we were studying, praying or sleeping. No one was supposed to violate a "BUSY" sign.

At 1:59 P.M. I hung out the "BUSY" sign.

The closet was too small to turn around in, so I backed into it, faced north, knelt down and closed the door. It was impossible to stand and close the door.

The closet was inky black. The heavy oak door fit snugly. Because I was facing the north end of the closet, I could not see the traces of light under the door.

The silence gripped me. I was more alone than I had ever been. The sounds of normal afternoon dormitory life could not penetrate the thick masonry walls. The clothes in the closet absorbed any noise that happened to leak in around the edges of the door. I had entered a world of silence.

I was more alone with God than I had ever been in my life. I closed my eyes to pray, but that was not necessary. The black closet was just as dark whether my eyes were open or shut. I wondered if God was in the blackness. I wondered if God would meet me there. I almost wanted to say,

"Hello God...are you there?"

I had been raised in a Presbyterian Sunday School, so I knew how to be reverent when I entered the church sanctuary. I had heard many prayers in that little Presbyterian church. So I began,

"Dear Father...."

TOUCHING GOD IN THE DARKNESS

I prayed in that dark closet just the way I had done in all my other prayers, trying to connect with God. I jumped right into the list of things I wanted from Him or the things I wanted Him to do for me. If I had known the formula of the Lord's Prayer, I would have worshiped God first. I was young, though, and people who have a childish spirit run to their Father and ask,

"What'd ya' bring me?" Children are always asking for something.

Little did I know then that when you only *ask* for things, you cut short your prayer time. We can only beg for things for so long.

After praying for a long time, my knees began to hurt. I rocked from one knee to the other. Because I was skinny, my knees were bony. The ache in my kneecaps was my first distraction from prayer. I wished I had put a small rug or towel on the floor. I even wished for some dirty socks to kneel on to ease the pain.

Returning to my prayer list, I forgot about my pain. I prayed intently through more requests. I felt I was talking to God. I felt he was listening to me.

As I got toward the end of my prayer list, I wondered about the time. I checked my watch, but could not see the hands. That was before the days of luminous watches. Although my eyes were not dilated, I could see nothing. Questioning the time was my second distraction.

Because my mind was fresh, I decided to pray all the way through my list of requests again...no matter how long it took. If I had to, I would stay much longer than one hour.

When I finished praying through my list a second time, I continued talking to God about things in general. Then my mind wandered to sports...to classes...to girls. I began to think about softball and found myself wanting to be on the athletic field. I came to myself, shook my head and realized I was not praying. Thinking about softball was my third distraction.

I decided to pray through my list a third time. This time I prayed through the list much faster. I did not want to miss the evening meal.

When I had nothing else to pray about, I decided to end my prayer. I was certain I had spent the large part of the afternoon in the closet. It was small, so I had to open the door and back out.

I blinked...rubbed my eyes...then massaged my aching knees. Walking over to the bedside table, I picked up the small travel clock I had received as a high school graduation gift. I could not believe my eyes. I put it to my ear to see if the clock was still ticking. It was.

I had prayed only 17 minutes.

This was a blow to my young male ego. I knew I could run faster or farther than anyone in college. All I had to do was make up my mind and force myself to do it. I felt I could do anything I set my mind to do. I had set my mind to pray one hour, but had only prayed 17 minutes. I was deflated at my failure.

HOW ARE YOU DOING IN YOUR PRAYER LIFE?

Now let's talk about you. Where are you in your walk with God? Maybe you never think at all about prayer. Begin by praying the Lord's Prayer. It only takes a minute. Maybe you dream of praying all day, or of spending one hour with God, but you just do not have the time. You just never get around to praying one hour. Do not try to do too much. Begin with the Lord's Prayer. You are doing what Jesus commanded. You can start with a one-minute prayer.

My professor in the spirituality class had given me an assignment to pray for one hour. The only place in the Bible that tells us how long to pray comes from that question Jesus asked, "Could ye not watch with me one hour?"

Notice that Jesus did not command people to *pray* for an hour. He spoke about *watching* for one hour. Maybe there is a difference between *watching* and *praying* for an hour. A few people can pray for one hour, but this book is not written to help you pray long prayers. I have written this book to help you talk to God. You can pray the Lord's Prayer in one minute, and if prayed properly that one minute can change your life.

Praying the Lord's Prayer is not about how long we pray. As a point of focus, just before Jesus told His disciples to pray the words of the Lord's Prayer, He said:

> When ye pray, use not vain repetitions, as the heathen do: for they think that they shall be heard for their much speaking (Matt. 6:7).

In this command, Jesus warns against two things. First, he does not want us just to repeat the words of any prayer again and again. Second, He does not want us to think the Father hears us simply because we talk to Him in long speeches. The effective prayer is not measured by how loud you pray, or how long you pray, or even if you say the words of the Lord's Prayer again and again in repetitious fashion. Your prayer will be effective if you are sincere (your approach) and if you ask for the right things (what you say).

Even when you don't pray the Lord's Prayer, and you don't rightly approach God, your prayers may provide what you need. Jesus tells us, "Your Father knoweth what things ye have need of, before ye ask him" (Matt. 6:8).

There is another reason, as a college freshman in that closet, I prayed only 17 minutes when I thought I had prayed for one or two hours. It had to do with what I was saying in prayer. I had gone to God praying through a grocery list of needs, and I ran through the list quickly. Prayers can become mechanical when you just pray for a list of people and things. On the other hand, if I had begun with *worship*, I possibly would never have run out of things to say. There is so much about God to praise that you could just keep going and going—just like the Energizer Bunny.

HOW TO BEGIN PRAISING GOD

Try thanking God for all He has done in your life.
Try worshiping God for all He has created.
Try praising God for all He has done,
especially as recorded in the Bible.
Try magnifying God for all you have in Christ.

Learning to talk to God by repeating the Lord's Prayer will help in all your praying. The Lord's Prayer will teach you to begin worshiping God as you talk to Him.

Babies run to a parent because they need something. As they grow into adulthood, they learn to talk to their parents, to understand them and to realize that love is reciprocal. As we mature spiritually, we learn to communicate with our heavenly Father and listen to Him.

Some days I get hung up on the first petition, and spend most of my prayer time repeating "Hallowed be thy name." I wrote the book *My Father's Names* (Regal Books, 1991), a work that lists more than 120 names of God. One day I prayed through the appendix of that book, which listed every name of God. I thanked God for every name and what it meant to me. It took me more than one hour just to worship Him by hallowing all His many names.

Some people try to pray for one hour, or for a long time, but often their minds go blank. When they do not know what to say, their minds wander to their jobs, television or something that worries them. The blank mind thinking about nothing causes the body to go to sleep. That is why many people start praying, but soon fall asleep.

God knows our weaknesses, and one of the reasons He gave us the Lord's Prayer was to help us pray...to keep us from going to sleep...to keep our minds focused on praying...to give us success in our prayers.

The monk in the monastery can spend one hour praying each day, or much longer. It only takes one minute to touch God, though, and to be touched by Him.

Most Americans, however, can't even pray for one minute.

Although most people are paid for working 40 hours a week, statistics tell us it will take approximately 54 hours of time out of our schedule to spend 40 hours in work. That is considering commuting to and from the job, lunchtime, work and phone calls from home, and other job-related necessities. This means we have less time than ever before—we are all busy.

> Time is the currency
> of today's world.

That means time is more valuable to most Americans than money.

You can pray the Lord's Prayer as you drive the expressway or as you ride to or from work on an elevated train.

Because you can pray the Lord's Prayer in one minute, why don't you make it the first thing you do when you sit down at your desk each day?

You may dream about praying one hour as I tried to do as a college freshman. You may dream about the benefits of talking to God for a longer time. By continually waiting to pray one hour, though, you will likely put off praying at all.

Begin with what you can do.

> It is very probable
> that the dream of the impossible
> becomes a barrier of the actual,
> that keeps you from doing what is possible.

THREE LEVELS OF THE LORD'S PRAYER

There are three levels to praying the Lord's Prayer.

First there is the *lip level*, which means you let your petitions flow over your lips, whether softly spoken or prayed out loud. The lip level focuses your mind and body.

The second dimension is the *mind level*, when you pray the Lord's Prayer inwardly. Pray the Lord's Prayer between sales, or when you are doing a task that requires no thought—whenever your mind belongs to you.

Third there is the *heart level*. This is the cry of passion or deep love. Heart prayer is usually done privately because the face reflects the heart. You should not cry, laugh or smile in an inappropriate place. Your business associates, for example, would not understand.

It is important to pray the Lord's Prayer at all three levels. When you meet alone with God, or in your church with others, pray aloud. At other times, pray it inwardly. God, who knows your thoughts, will hear your request. For those special occasions when only you and God are present, pray passionately with your heart.

Decide now to begin praying the Lord's Prayer tomorrow morning when the alarm rings. Then as you commute to work, or during work, pray the Lord's Prayer at least once, perhaps more.

Begin spending a few minutes with God today. Begin with the Lord's Prayer. If you have the privacy of your bedroom or a private family room, open your Bible to Matthew 6:9-13. Then, following the words Jesus gave us, pray the Lord's Prayer...slowly...reverently...and meaningfully. Do not give a speech to God. Do not just read words from a book. Tell God what each of the seven petitions means to you, and what you want Him to do for you.

Develop a pattern for prayer. Instead of automatically turning on the radio when you get into your car each day to go to work, pray the Lord's Prayer. Maybe you need strength in a particular place in your life. That could be the place to start.

An office manager once told me almost everything about her career was wonderful. She said she did a good job, she was satisfied with her production and she felt comfortable managing those for whom she was responsible. The only thing she hated about her job was when she was called into the plant manager's office. He was perpetually grouchy. He always saw the problems and complained. He never saw the growing efficiency charts.

"Pray the Lord's Prayer on the way to his office," I told her. I suggested she pray that God's name be hallowed in their plant, that God's kingdom come and that God's will be done. She accepted my advice.

"It changed me," she said.

Praying the Lord's Prayer took away her fear and gave her new boldness. Instead of being defensive with her plant manager, she became positive.

"Let me help you get a better perspective," she told her plant manager.

"I got faith from the Lord's Prayer," she said. "It gave me courage to aggressively suggest new ways for him to look at things. Now I always say the Lord's Prayer walking from my desk to his office," was her testimony.

We need to look for places to pray the Lord's Prayer other than those where we have daily problems. We need to look for times such as waiting for the bus, waiting at the copier or other downtimes when our thoughts belong to us.

> The secret of your future
> lies in your daily routine.

Determine to pray the Lord's Prayer each day at approximately the same time and place. Get in the habit of talking to God about your life.

SEVEN RESULTS TO EXPECT

If you pray the Lord's Prayer daily, you will receive seven things that will change your life and redirect your future.

First, you will magnify God each day, which means you are praying, "Hallowed be Thy name." As you worship God each day, you grow as a Christian because you are learning about Him...you are becoming comfortable around Him...you learn what He expects of you.

God rewards you with His presence. "Anyone who comes to him must believe that he exists and that he rewards those who earnestly seek him" (Heb. 11:6, *NIV*). Your reward for praying the Lord's Prayer daily is more than money. God rewards you with Himself...His assurance...and His guidance.

When I was a kid, I would greet my father at the door asking the child's typical question: "What'd ya' bring me?"

My father would always reply, "Myself."

I did not fully appreciate his response until I met kids from single-parent homes who did not have a father who comes home every night.

Second, you will live by better principles when you pray the Lord's Prayer. When you pray "Thy kingdom come," you are asking for God to bring His kingdom principles and kingdom agenda into your life. You will have a better life when you live by God's rules...when you obey them...because you love them and the rule giver. You will prosper from living by these principles. You will grow to be like God when you honestly pray, "Thy kingdom come in my life on earth as Your kingdom reigns in heaven."

Third, God will guide you for that day. When you pray "Thy will be done," you are asking God to guide you into His plan and purpose for your life.

The *fourth* result of praying the Lord's Prayer each day is receiving more answers from God. The pro golfer Lee Trevino held up a golf ball in a commercial and boasted, "This ball will take strokes off your game."

"Wow!" I thought. "I've gotta get some."

Then Lee Trevino laughed displaying a playful smile and said, "This golf ball will take strokes off your golf game, but you've gotta hit it 300 times a day."

The secret is not the ball. The secret is practice...practice...practice. Not just hitting the ball a lot. The irony is that you have to hit it continually and correctly until you learn how to hit it correctly and continually!

The Lord's Prayer is like a golf ball. Just praying it one time won't get you answers. Or, to use golf vernacular, it won't take strokes off the game of life.

You have to pray correctly...with all your heart...according to the will of God...according to God's formula. When you do that, you will receive answers. To pray it one time, though, is not enough. You have to pray correctly and continually to receive answers.

Fifth, you feel clean when you pray the Lord's Prayer. When you ask God "Forgive us our debts...," you not only receive forgiveness, but you also know immediately that you *are* forgiven. You experience forgiveness. You feel forgiven.

If I paid off your credit-card bill, your debt would be forgiven on the computer. You would owe nothing. If I did not tell you about it, however, you would still "feel" in debt. When you think your debt is too high, you do not charge anything else on your card. Your feelings about debt keep you in bondage to the debt.

You need two things to be free. First you need to be out of debt, and second you need to *feel* financially free. When you properly pray the Lord's Prayer, you can be free of sin, and feel it.

The *sixth* thing the Lord's Prayer gives you is victory. Everyone wants to rise above circumstances and be victorious over problems. When you pray "Lead us not into temptation...," you ask God to keep you from situations that would destroy you.

The last and *seventh* petition gives you protection. When you pray "Deliver us from the evil one," you receive from God a protective shield around your life.

KEEPING A PRAYER JOURNAL

Some who are serious about talking to God keep a journal. It is something like kids keeping a diary at camp—a record of their experiences, both good and bad, and their impressions. Each chapter in this book will include suggestions about what experiences and impressions regarding your prayers you should write.

This chapter discusses the length of prayer and the place of prayer. Let the following questions guide your journal entries.

1. How effective are your short prayers? If you can't get into the spirit of prayer in one minute, say so. Write your impressions of what prayer does to you.
2. Where is it most effective to pray? Least effective?
3. What is happening to you because you pray the Lord's Prayer several times each day?

The following "Prayer Checklist" is another way to use your prayer journal.

PRAYER CHECKLIST

Where or when you pray	How are you doing? (check one)		
	Lousy	Average	Great
1. When I first get up			
2. At regular private prayer times			
3. On the way to or from work			
(Other:)			

THREE-STEP BIBLE STUDY

WHERE AND HOW LONG TO PRAY

Another regular feature in this book is a Three-Step Bible Study. In Step 1, read the question, and think about how you might answer it. Step 2 consists of reading the Bible verse printed in the box to discover how the Word of God answers the question. In Step 3, write the answer in the space provided.

1. What is a good time of day for you to begin praying, and why then?

"O God, You are my God; early will I seek You; my soul thirsts for You; my flesh longs for You in a dry and thirsty land where there is no water."—Psalm 63:1 *(NKJV)*

_____

_____

_____

2. What other times of day can you pray the Lord's Prayer? What time is best for you?

> "Evening, and morning, and at noon, will I pray, and cry aloud: and he shall hear my voice."—Psalm 55:17

_____

_____

_____

_____

3. What are the benefits of a fixed time for prayer? Notice how Daniel had regular times for prayer. What would this do for you? (Read Daniel 6:1-24.)

> "When Daniel knew that the writing was signed, he went into his house; and his windows being open in his chamber toward Jerusalem, he kneeled upon his knees three times a day, and prayed, and gave thanks before his God, as he did aforetime."—Daniel 6:10

_____

_____

_____

4. What can be your response in times of danger or discouragement?

> "And when they had laid many stripes on them, they threw them into prison, commanding the jailer to keep them securely. Having received such a charge, he put them into the inner prison and fastened their feet in the stocks. But at midnight Paul and Silas were praying and singing hymns to God, and the prisoners were listening to them."
> —Acts 16:23-25 *(NKJV)*

_____

_____

_____

_____

5. How should you respond in prayer to opportunity?

> "The king said unto me, For what dost thou make request? So I prayed to the God of heaven. And I said unto the king..."—Nehemiah 2:4,5

---

6. When can you stop praying?

> "Pray without ceasing."—1 Thessalonians 5:17

---

7. What things should be on your prayer list?

> "But in every thing by prayer and supplication with thanksgiving let your requests be made known unto God."—Philippians 4:6

---

8. For whom should you pray? Why?

> "I exhort therefore, that, first of all, supplications, prayers, intercessions, and giving of thanks, be made for all men; for kings, and for all that are in authority."—1 Timothy 2:1,2

Feelings from the Lord's Prayer

Our...Family feeling
Father...Intimate feeling
Hallowed be thy name...Reverent feeling
Thy kingdom come...Majestic feeling
Thy will be done...Submissive feeling
Give us bread...Reliant feeling
Forgive us our debt...Cleansed feeling
Lead us not into temptation...Victorious feeling
Deliver us from the evil one...Triumphant feeling
Thine is the kingdom...Dependent feeling
And the power...Magnificent feeling
And the glory...Exalted feeling
Amen...Completed feeling

BEGINNING TO PRAY:
APPROACH GOD RIGHT

Call God Your Father

My wife and I were standing on the boardwalk at Myrtle Beach, South Carolina, when I felt a tug on my right pocket. I looked down to see a little guy tugging on my yellow windbreaker pocket. He was not looking at me, though. His eyes were fastened intently on the swirling, fluffy, pink cotton candy in the vendor's stall. Pointing to the cotton candy, he asked,

"Can I have some...?"

My wife, Ruth, was also watching the vendor twist the paper cone to lift cotton candy out of the swirling sugar.

"Please...can I have some?" the black-headed little guy kept asking.

I smiled to myself, knowing what was happening. I am a grandfather who likes to buy children goodies. I would have been happy to buy this boy some gooey cotton candy. He was irresistible, his black hair hanging in bangs over his forehead. The Chicago Cubs T-shirt was too big and his brown skin suggested Hispanic descent. He was someone else's child, though.

"Please..." the words trailed off.

"OK..." I finally answered.

Hearing me speak, the boy suddenly pulled his hand away. He did not recognize my voice.

"Big or little?" I asked, looking down at him.

He bashfully shrugged his shoulders, one hand holding the fingers of the other. He had just begged, "Please..." but now I could not get him to talk.

Then the boy's father, who had seen what happened, came through the crowd. It was easy to see how the little boy had mistaken me for his father. We both wore similar yellow windbreakers. Although I still offered to buy the pink cotton candy, the father insisted on paying for it himself.

This scene on the boardwalk at Myrtle Beach can teach us at least three lessons about prayer.

First, everyone who tugs on the pocket of our heavenly Father is not His child.

Second, God wants to do things for everyone, but can't because all are not His children.

Third, when you become a child of God, you can receive "cotton candy" from Him.

Jesus taught us a new way to address God. He taught us to call God "Our Father," and He told us that we could have a unique relationship with this heavenly Father.

My father was a drinking man, and I have some unpleasant memories because of his alcoholism. We had one relationship, however, that is still special to me. Just about every Saturday he gave me a quarter to go to the movies.

My father worked as a clerk at White Hardware Company for 42 years. Mother went downtown on Saturday evening when he got paid to receive her share, or else she would not have had the money needed to run the house. He would have spent it all on liquor. They always fussed about money; but my father liked to give me a quarter for the movies.

We lived about two miles from the heart of downtown Savannah, Georgia, and it took about an hour to walk the distance. I crossed a pasture, jumped a couple of creeks and cut through the historical district to Drayton and St. Julian Streets where the hardware store was located. I walked up to my dad and said, "I want a quarter for the movies."

He never tried to give me less, or to hold back, which would have been understandable. It only cost a dime to get into the matinee. He could have given me just a dime for the movies. He always gave me a dime for the movies and a nickel for popcorn, a nickel for a Dr. Pepper and a nickel for a candy bar. My dad wanted me to have a great time, so he always gave me a quarter.

He never gave me more than a quarter—maybe because I never asked. I always just said, "I want a quarter for the movies."

I still see my dad taking a handful of change out of his pocket. Holding the change down by his pocket because he was nearsighted, he put a finger to his mouth as he studied the coins. He must have been counting them. Then he took a quarter out of his palm, handed it to me and said, "Here. Have a good time."

I never once got halfway to town and questioned whether my father would give me a quarter. He always had done it, so I always expected it. He never once turned me down. A couple of times when I got there before he got his paycheck, he borrowed a quarter to give to me.

It never once occurred to me to ask for more or less than a quarter. I asked for what I knew my father wanted to give. I asked for a quarter.

We should have the same relationship with our heavenly Father. We should ask for what we know He will give, we should ask in faith and we should take the initiative to go to Him.

When you begin praying the Lord's Prayer, "Our Father which art in heaven," you are following the revolutionary approach to prayer that Jesus taught. This new title for God that is included in the Lord's Prayer suggests the following ideas:

FOUR ESSENTIALS ABOUT GOD FROM THE LORD'S PRAYER

1. The God of heaven is a Father
2. The Father allows immediate access to Himself
3. I can have an intimate relationship with the Father
4. The Lord's Prayer is a special means of approaching God as Father

---

I listen to the way people begin their prayers. It tells me a lot about the way they think. When someone begins "Dear God...," it tells me that God is impersonal to that person. When someone prays "Dear Lord...," the person acknowledges God's power, but still He is impersonal. "Dear So-and-So" is the way we start a letter to someone, even if we don't know the person.

Once I went to a prayer meeting just to hear the prayer of Dr. W. A. Criswell, former and beloved pastor of First Baptist Church of Dallas, Texas. He knelt, reverently lifted his face to heaven as though he were looking into the face of God. Then he began simply, "Master...." That was his favorite name for God.

My favorite name for God is different. Of all the names people use to address God, I like best the name "Father."

THE GOD OF HEAVEN IS A FATHER

The Old Testament Jews did not think of God as an intimate Father. He was the Lord God Almighty, the One who "dwellest between the cherubims" (Ps. 80:1). He was the God who came down to earth in the Shekinah Glory Cloud, a whirlwind of fire as bright and awesome as any display of power Israel had ever seen, a fearful God exacting punishment on the transgressor.

God told Moses, "Lo, I come unto thee in a thick cloud, that the people may hear when I speak with thee" (Exod. 19:9). When God came to Mount Sinai, He warned, "Take heed to yourselves, that ye go not up into the mount, or touch the border of it: whosoever toucheth the mount shall be surely put to death" (v. 12).

The Lord God of the Old Testament was to be feared because He killed Uzzah when he reached out and touched the Ark of the Covenant (see 2 Sam. 6:6).

The Lord God of the Old Testament was to be feared because He punished Moses for disobedience, so that Moses never entered the Promised Land (see Num. 20:7-13).

The Lord God of the Old Testament was to be feared because He allowed Nebuchadnezzar to destroy Jerusalem because the Jews worshiped idols and committed fornication (see 2 Chron. 36:15-21).

Even the New Testament portrays God in His judgmental nature: "Our God is a consuming fire" (Heb. 12:29).

Jesus, however, came teaching us to call God by a new name. He told His followers to say, when they prayed, "Our Father." Jesus gave them a new revelation about the Lord God of Israel. God was no longer far off. He could be approached as an intimate Father.

Jesus Himself called God Father. He said, "I am the way, the truth, and the life: no man cometh unto the Father, but by me" (John 14:6). Jesus promised we could get close to the Father, like a little girl cuddling up in her daddy's lap. Just as a father takes a storybook and reads to her, so we can be intimate with the Father.

A little boy asks for cotton candy on the boardwalk, and his daddy buys some for him. Why? Because they have a relationship. The father loves the son, and the little boy trusts the father...he trusts him so much that he can ask him for cotton candy.

Asking God for personal things is not as strong a theme in the Old Testament as it is in the New. The Old Testament Jews brought their blood sacrifices to the altar at the door to the Tabernacle. They killed the best of their lambs as a sacrifice for sin, for "without shedding of blood is no remission" (Heb. 9:22). The Old Testament Jews came fearfully to God because they knew the sinfulness of their hearts.

Jesus, however, changed the way people came to God. Jesus is "The Lamb of God, which taketh away the sin of the world" (John 1:29). So we come to Jesus for forgiveness. We are accepted in Jesus, who told us, "Him that cometh to me I will in no wise cast out" (6:37).

How do you believe in Jesus? John, the Gospel writer, said, "But as many as received Him [Jesus], to them He gave the right to become children of God, to those who believe in His name" (John 1:12, *NKJV*). We become God's children and enter God's family when we believe in Jesus. When you become a child of God, you can call Him Father.

When you ask Jesus into your life, you ask God to cleanse you of sin because of the sacrifice of His Son...you ask Him to give you peace...you ask Him to take control of your living. You ask God all this because He is now your Father. This is the new name Jesus gave to the Lord God Almighty. Jesus called Him Father.

Now, I am a father and my children call me affectionately, "Dad." They don't call me Father to my face. They use that title only when talking to other people. The word "father" is really a title. Any man who has children has the title "father." My *name* is Elmer Towns; my *title* is "father."

The term "Father" is one of the *names* of the first Person of the

Trinity. His name is more than a title. Jesus said, "I am come in my Father's name" (John 5:43). Jesus prayed, "O righteous Father, the world hath not known thee: but I have known thee" (17:25). Then Jesus explains, "I have declared unto them thy name" (v. 26).

You can get to know other things about me by my other titles. I am called "Professor" at Liberty University because I teach students. I am also Dean of the School of Religion because I administer faculty. I also have the title "Reverend" because I was ordained and set apart for ministry. Sometimes people refer to me as Dr. Towns, in recognition of my academic degree. In my first church they called me "Preacher" because I was too young to be called Reverend and too immature to be called Pastor. The only thing I did well was preach, so they called me "Preacher." My children call me "Dad," my wife calls me "Honey" and my grandchildren call me "Doc," another term of endearment. Each title I wear like a hat, and each title tells who I am and the things I do.

God has many names and titles. You could call Him God... Almighty...the Lord of Host...Rock...or even Jehovah Rapha (the Lord, our Healer). God has many titles, and each title reveals a different task He does for His people. He is the Lord of Hosts, which means He is God of the fighting angels, and He is Jehovah Rohi, The Lord Is My Shepherd. He is El Shaddai, the One Who Is More Than Enough to Meet Our Needs. The more we understand His many titles, the more we understand what He does for us.

None of God's many names and titles, though, is as intimate as His name, Father. When God is our Father, we can say with Paul, "We cry, Abba Father" (Rom. 8:15). The Greek word for father is *pater*. In this verse, however, Paul precedes the word *pater* with the word *abba*, which is an Aramaic word, the spoken language of Jesus, Paul and others who lived in Palestine. Jesus also called God "Abba, Father" (Mark 14:36).

The word *abba* was a colloquial term of endearment, like the terms "Papa" or "Daddy" for us. Jesus and Paul are telling us we can use intimate terms of endearment with the Father. God is a Father who is near and dear to us.

When we pray "Our Father," we are also suggesting that a world of people do not know God as their Father. Jesus told the Pharisees of His day, "If God were your Father, ye would love me" (John 8:42).

Obviously the Pharisees hated Jesus, for they had previously tried to kill Him. Finally they would succeed in getting Roman soldiers to nail Him to a cross. However, Jesus knew the hearts of the Pharisees. He said to them, "Ye are of your father the devil" (v. 44).

There are two families in the world. There is the family of God, in which His children call Him Father. Then there is the family of the world—children who cannot call God their Father. The children of the world cannot effectively pray the Lord's Prayer until they come to the Father by Jesus. Then they can get results to their prayers when they say, "Our Father."

However, we need to stop and talk about those who can't pray the Lord's Prayer. In one sense, they are the children of God because He created them, as He did all people. Therefore, all people are children of God by creation. In this sense Paul explains, "If haply they might feel after him [the Father], and find him, though he be not far from every one of us: for in him we live, and move, and have our being" (Acts 17:27,28).

We learn from this statement that all are God's children by virtue of His having created us; and that God is close to people—close enough that they only need to reach out and receive Him into their lives.

THE FATHER ALLOWS
IMMEDIATE ACCESS TO HIMSELF

You can pray anywhere, "Our Father which art in heaven." You can be on a break in the cafeteria, or driving the expressway. You can be jogging, or riding your mower cutting the grass. No matter where you are praying, you have immediate access to the throne room of heaven.

Obviously, this does not mean you travel through space. Nor are you transported in a trance or vision. Your physical body stays where you are, but your prayers enter into God's throne room. Your prayers enter heaven. You pray "Our Father which art in heaven," and you have His attention. God in heaven hears you.

God is everywhere. He is inside the smallest atom, for "by him all things are held together" (Col. 1:17, author's translation), and He upholds "all things by the word of his power" (Heb. 1:3). God also inhabits the farthest star: "If I ascend up into heaven, thou art there"

(Ps. 139:8). God is everywhere, which means God is *there*. So no matter where you are, God hears you.

God is near you...over you...around you...and inside you. So He can hear everything you pray. When you pray out loud, God hears because He is there, even while He is in heaven. When you pray inwardly, He hears because "thou understandest my thought" (Ps. 139:2).

When you pray on the jogging path, God can hear your prayers because "thou [God] compassest my path" (v. 3). When you first wake in the morning to pray the Lord's Prayer while still under the covers, God hears because "thou [God] compassest...my lying down" (v. 3).

You can pray the Lord's Prayer when you are scared, just as a little boy runs into his daddy's room at night because of a threatening thunderstorm. Just as the father tucks his child into bed, so you can have immediate access to the heavenly Father.

You can run to your heavenly Father when you are glad, like the little kid who gets up early in the morning, hears his parents talking and runs and jumps on his father's bed to get in on the fun. Dad rollicks with him in the covers and they laugh together. Just as the earthly father welcomes his child, so our heavenly Father lets us run into His presence any time for fellowship.

The new name, "Father," that Jesus gave us for God means we have a new and immediate access to Him, just as we have with a loving Daddy.

I CAN HAVE AN INTIMATE RELATIONSHIP WITH THE FATHER

Jesus promised us a new and intimate relationship with Him and the Father. Jesus prayed, "That they all [all believers] may be one; as thou, Father, art in me, and I in thee, that they also may be one in us" (John 17:21).

Jesus did not mean that we lose our identity and consciousness in God. We are in God and He is in us, but we are still two separate persons. Jesus was explaining that we can have an intimate relationship with the Father.

Because of our intimacy with God, Jesus told us to address Him, "Our Father."

Jesus could have told us, "When you pray, say, 'O God.'" That would have shown His absolute power over us. But Jesus wanted us to know something more than God's awesome power.

Jesus could have told us, "When you pray, say 'My Lord.'" That would have shown His sovereignty over us. Jesus, however, wanted us to know something more than God's control of our lives.

Jesus could have told us, "When you pray, say 'Dear Master.'" In Jesus' day, that term meant "teacher," and this would have shown God's guidance. Jesus, however, wanted to show more than the way the Master directs and guides our lives.

Jesus could have told us, "When you pray, say 'My Shepherd.'" That would have shown His care over us. Jesus, however, wanted to show that God offers us greater protection than a shepherd's care for his animals.

Jesus could have told us, "When you pray, say 'Hail, King!'" That would have shown God's rule over us. Jesus, however, wanted to show a better way for us to relate to God.

Instead of these terms, Jesus chose to use one that speaks of a more intimate relationship with God. Jesus told us to call God, "Our Father."

When you begin to pray, you are like a little child of a king, who walks right into the presence of his father. The guards do not stop the boy, and none of the executive staff interferes. He is the king's child. He has immediate access to the king because they are related. The king is the child's father. When you pray "Our Father," you know that you belong to God, and that He belongs to you. You are related.

What is the relationship of Father to child? It is a relationship of *intimacy*.

How do you feel when you are intimate with someone...parent, spouse, friend, or brother or sister? When you are intimate, you feel at *one* with them. You feel together, you think together, you love the same things and you like to go places together. Intimacy is *oneness*.

The Lord's Prayer offers you that kind of oneness with God.

THE LORD'S PRAYER IS A SPECIAL MEANS OF APPROACHING THE FATHER

Have you ever thought why the Lord's Prayer begins, "Our Father"? Why not just speak of God as *a* Father? Jesus could have compared our relationship with God to a relationship a child has with an earthly father. Jesus, however, did not call God "a Father."

Jesus could have called God *the* Father. The article "the" would have pointed out the uniqueness of God the Father. It would have meant that God is the only Father. But Jesus didn't call God *the* Father, at least in this prayer.

Jesus could have told us to get God's attention by calling out, "Oh, God!" A Hollywood movie by that title was popular in the 1970s. We do not have to begin our prayers by saying "Oh, God," as though He is sleeping and needs to be awakened. Neither is He on a weekend vacation. He is here, and He has our attention.

Why did Jesus tell His disciples to use the plural pronoun "our" when addressing God? Why did He introduce this prayer, "Our Father"? Was it because the disciples as a group asked Jesus, "Teach us to pray" (Luke 11:1), so Jesus gave a them a corporate or group prayer they could use as a Body? That would mean the 12 apostles could gather and begin praying together, "Our Father."

Some people think the Lord's Prayer has the plural pronouns *our*, *us* and *we* because it should be prayed in a group, as congregations today pray corporately the Lord's Prayer.

All these views are interesting, but notice who is teaching the disciples how to pray: it is Jesus. He taught us to pray, "Our Father." Those who heard what Jesus said realized He was inviting them to join Him in prayer. He meant for us to pray with Him.

When I proposed to Ruth, I told her about where we would live. I called it "our home." Of course I meant that the house would belong to both of us. Now the title deed has both our names and signatures on it. So the phrase "our house" means that the place belongs to my wife and me.

When you pray "Our Father," the plural pronoun means you are coming with Jesus to the Father. Although it is appropriate to pray the Lord's Prayer along with others in a public worship service, God does not hear your prayers just because you come with others, even if the others are more godly than you. God hears your prayers because you come with Jesus Christ.

When you come to God praying "Our Father," it is like saying, "We—Jesus and I—are coming in prayer." Because Jesus is in my heart, it is "both of us."

Jesus told His disciples, "Whatsoever ye shall ask in my name, that will I do" (John 14:13). So most of our prayers end with the conclusion, "In Jesus' name."

We do not end the Lord's Prayer by using the phrase, "In Jesus' name." I have never heard anyone add that to the end of the Lord's Prayer. Why?

Because when we begin the Lord's Prayer saying "Our Father" we are including in that introduction the same idea as the usual conclusion, "In Jesus' name." Both phrases mean that our prayer is based on Jesus' righteousness, not our own. God the Father will hear our prayers because they are based on the righteousness of Jesus Christ His Son. Our prayers are not based on our ability to pray, or our sincerity.

When we come to the Father with Jesus Christ, we come through His blood that gives us access to Him. Paul describes this process: "For through him [Christ] we...have access by one Spirit unto the father" (Eph. 2:18).

Many prayers are recorded in the Bible, and each one has different words by which to approach God and different titles by which to call Him. Many were great prayers because of their great answers. The Lord's Prayer, however, is the greatest prayer, taught to us by the greatest Person for the greatest breadth of requests, and who has the greatest title for God. Because there is simplicity in greatness, when you pray, say, "Our Father which art in heaven"—the simplest prayer that has the greatest influence.

PRAYER CHECKLIST			
How do you approach and address God?	**How are you doing? (check one)**		
	Lousy	*Average*	*Great*
1.			
2.			
3.			
4.			
5.			

JOURNALING

Each day you will approach the Father in a different way. You will have different needs, different moods and different circumstances. Write how you approached God in a previous prayer. Later, when you review the various ways you approached God, you will broaden your understanding of how to come to God. Obviously, we all come to the Father through Jesus Christ, but we apply it differently.

1. What do you mean by the word *our* in "Our Father"?
2. What does the name "Father" mean to you? For your understanding of God? For the way you approach Him?
3. Describe your experience in prayer for each day's approach to God.
4. What does praying the Lord's Prayer do to your feelings? Thinking? Actions?

THREE-STEP BIBLE STUDY

I BELIEVE IN GOD THE FATHER ALMIGHTY

The title of this Bible study is taken from the first line of the Apostles' Creed. It states that the Almighty God of the Old Testament is our Father. Step 1—Read the question to get you thinking about the meaning of the Lord's Prayer. Step 2—Study the verses to determine their meaning. Step 3—Write your answers in the space provided.

1. Note the first recorded words of Christ in Scripture. His parents have lost Him in the Temple in Jerusalem. He was 12 years old. When His parents found Jesus, they asked where He had been. What do we know about the relationship between Jesus and God from His answer?

> "And He [Jesus] said to them, 'Why did you seek Me? Did you not know that I must be about My Father's business?'"—Luke 2:49 (NKJV)

_____

_____

_____

2. What privilege do you have because you are a child of God?

> "That which we have seen and heard declare we unto you, that ye also may have fellowship with us: and truly our fellowship is with the Father, and with his Son Jesus Christ."—1 John 1:3

_____

_____

_____

_____

3. What relationship do you have with the Father?

> "For ye have not received the spirit of bondage again to fear; but ye have received the Spirit of adoption, whereby we cry, Abba, Father."—Romans 8:15

_____

_____

_____

4. What assurance can you have from the Father?

> "Holy Father, keep through thine own name those whom thou hast given me, that they may be one, as we are." —John 17:11

_____

_____

_____

5. What can you get from the Father? What will this do for you?

> "That the God of our Lord Jesus Christ, the Father of glory, may give unto you the spirit of wisdom and revelation in the knowledge of him."—Ephesians 1:17

_____
_____
_____
_____

6. What does the Father give to His children?

> "Every good gift and every perfect gift is from above, and cometh down from the Father of lights, with whom is no variableness, neither shadow of turning."—James 1:17

_____
_____
_____
_____

7. What does the Father do for His own?

> "Jude, the servant of Jesus Christ, and brother of James, to them that are sanctified by God the Father, and preserved in Jesus Christ, and called."—Jude 1

_____
_____
_____
_____

8. What happens to your relationship with the Father if you sin?

"My little children, these things write I unto you, that ye sin not. And if any man sin, we have an advocate with the Father, Jesus Christ the righteous."—1 John 2:1

_____

_____

_____

_____

Relationships in the Lord's Prayer

Our Father...Father and child
Hallowed be thy name...God and worshiper
Thy Kingdom come...King and subject
Thy will be done...Master and servant
Give us bread...Provider and recipient
Forgive us our sins...Savior and sinner
Lead us not into temptation...Guide and follower
Deliver us from evil...Protector and Deliverer
For thine is the kingdom...Sovereign and subject

~⚬~ 3 ~⚬~

THE FIRST PETITION:
THY NAME BE HALLOWED

Worship Touches God

I almost missed one of the greatest worship experiences of my life.

I was speaking at the South Dakota Salvation Army offices near Rapid City, South Dakota. I arranged with my host officer to drive me to see the carvings of the presidents on Mount Rushmore after my evening message.

The trip would take 30 minutes from the lodge where we were staying, so I was told to cut my sermon short. However, I delved into my message and spoke a little longer than expected. I was told to leave immediately after my sermon, but some officers had questions. So I hung around to talk.

I was told the lights went out on Mount Rushmore at 11:00 P.M.

At 11:00 P.M., we were a couple of miles away. I could see the glare of the spotlights, the way one sees the lights of a city illuminate the sky at night.

Suddenly the horizon went dark.

"We'll see the presidents by moonlight," I said, and asked my host to keep driving.

We arrived at the reception center as visitors and workers were driving away. We followed the sidewalk around behind the reception center for a panoramic view of Washington, Jefferson, Lincoln and Roosevelt.

Suddenly a huge, black thundercloud covered the moon and we had difficulty following the sidewalk. The cloud was so dark that we could not see each other.

Just my luck, I thought. *I spoke too long, and now this black cloud covers my view.*

I was very disappointed. I felt I would probably never get back to Mount Rushmore again.

Then God intervened....

A bolt of silver lightning flashed behind Rushmore. For a moment I saw the white outline of four presidents' heads as the lightning lit up the western sky.

Then the sky fell black again. I could see nothing.

The lightning flashed again, though, and the entire sky overhead lit up like an electric spider web. Lightning ran across the horizon, and seemed to ignite lesser lights in every direction.

Again I saw the four faces.

"Do it again, God," I silently prayed.

He did.

Another gigantic splash of lightning spread out over the vast South Dakota sky, and for several seconds I could see each face clearly.

Then blackness settled again over Mount Rushmore. I could see nothing—not even the Salvation Army officers standing next to me.

I was standing reverently before God. I felt that the place was as holy as a church sanctuary one enters quietly. I could feel the majesty of God's presence. In that reverent atmosphere, I worshiped God.

That evening my sanctuary was the observation platform at Mount Rushmore. God's prompting was His lightning. I waited for another lightning flash so I could study the features of another president. Then I thought,

Just as I strain to see Rushmore, so we strain to see God in this black world of sin.

I realized that we see God quickly and momentarily, as though in lightning flashes. We never see Him perfectly and completely, though, because we are limited, while He is perfect.

How do I see God? I asked myself.

Then I answered my own question. I was not talking to the Salvation Army captain, because he was lost in his own thought world; it was to myself I thought:

I see God in the Bible....

In miracles....

In nature....

Then it dawned on me in that electrical storm in the Black Hills of South Dakota that *I see God in His many names....*

Each name of God is like a lightning flash that reveals something about God, just as I learned something about a president from the lightning that evening. As I tried to interpret the stone sculptures before me, I also tried to understand the God of heaven who was putting on a lightning show for me.

Hallowed be Your name, Creator God, I meditated, *for You created the Black Hills.*

Hallowed be Your name, Lord. I thought about His kindness to people.

Hallowed be Your name, Master. I submitted to His rulership as the Master of my life.

Hallowed be Your name, Almighty. I recognized His power in the flashing lightning and in the thunder rolling up the valleys.

Hallowed be Your name, Father. I praised Him for loving me and taking care of me.

The blackness between flashes of light seemed even blacker. Maybe it was because when we see God's light, everything else is night. Just as "night unto night sheweth knowledge" (Ps. 19:2), so the blackness of Rushmore illuminated for me the golden glow of God.

The lightning storm passed over Rushmore and the flashes became less frequent, but God is eternal light. I felt comfortable in the darkness because "The darkness he [God] called Night" (Gen. 1:5).

Now the lightning flickered only momentarily, and we could no longer see anything, even each other as we stood side by side. Inside my mind, though, I could see clearly. I could see God.

As we rode home in silence that evening, my host and I realized we had witnessed the best show Mount Rushmore could ever display. We had not seen the mountain through the eyes of the U.S. Park Service, but we saw it through God's eyes.

When you begin praying "Hallowed be Thy name," you recognize five truths about God.

> ## FIVE ESSENTIALS ABOUT HONORING GOD'S NAME
>
> 1. God has a name
> 2. God's name is holy
> 3. God wants us to praise Him
> 4. I can praise God's name with the Lord's Prayer
> 5. God will not force anyone to praise His name

When you know these five things about God's name, you can better approach Him in prayer. You need to approach God the way a salesman properly uses a customer's name...the way a boyfriend properly calls out the name of the one he loves...the way a mother tenderly teaches her child his or her name...the way a subject addresses the queen...the way God is important to you.

GOD HAS A NAME

My mother was a McFadden. She was proud of her name and heritage. When I was a little boy, she would take me to the McFadden's Family Cemetery near Sardinia, South Carolina. She had me stand in front of the large, 10-foot tall McFadden granite history stone that told how John McFadden came to the United States in 1730 to pioneer that part of South Carolina. Mother would preach to me, "Remember who you are." She reminded me, "Be proud of your name." Then to motivate me even more she would say, "Remember, you are a Towns...you can do anything you set your mind to."

So growing up, my family name was important to me. Although I studied McFadden history to know my grandparents on my mother's side better, the name she took in marriage became important to her...and to me. "Remember, you are a Towns."

When you hallow God's name, you esteem Him for who He is, not just reverence His title. When we say today, "That person has made a name for himself," we do not mean he has created a unique spelling of his name. We mean he has developed a reputation that stands behind his name. When we describe a person who has a "good name," we speak about a person who has a good reputation.

When you begin your prayer, "Our Father," you begin praying in an intimate relationship with God—that of a father and a child. God is not an angry judge waiting to punish you, nor is He aloof and ignoring you, nor is He too busy to hear you. God is not some far-off deity in heaven; He is your Father who can be approached on an intimate basis.

Prayer should be like a child jumping on a father's lap to say, "I love you."

The Lord's Prayer is therefore not just for you. It is also for God. Begin with "Hallowed be Thy name." Begin with God and His desire. He desires to be glorified.

The word "hallowed" should remind us of the "hallowed hills" of a university or a court building's "hallowed halls of justice." The word "hallowed" means respect that has grown during a period of time.

Why does someone hallow a precious gem? It is because the gem is expensive...it is one of a kind...it is passed from generation to generation...it has a history...it is given as an engagement promise of love and fidelity.

When you pray "Hallowed be Thy name," you recognize how meaningful God is to you and your life.

Some people pray "Hallowed be Thy name" the way they would say the statement "God save the queen," or "God bless America." They think it is as if an American is saluting the flag, or someone is crossing him- or herself in front of the altar, or two gentlemen are shaking hands when they meet. When Jesus told us to pray "Hallowed be Thy name," however, He used such a rich, full, exhaustive phrase that it is almost impossible to explain with human words. Jesus knew we were human, though, so He was stretching us to aspire to a new level of worship.

When you pray "Hallowed be Thy name," you climb to a new level of respect for God and reverence for His person. You are ascending into the very heart of God to recognize who He is, and what He has done for us.

What is in a name? Because we give so little meaning to names, we must look at names as the Hebrews use them to understand this phrase.

God has three primary names in the Old Testament.

God's first name is *Elohim* (i.e., God the Mighty Creator). By using this name we say, "In the beginning God created the heaven and the earth" (Gen. 1:1).

God's second name is *Yahweh*, which means, "The Lord who is the covenant-keeping One."

Then God has a third name, *Adonai*, which means "Master" or "Lord." As our Master, God is the one who rules our lives. So there are three primary names for God, but only one God: "The Lord our God is one Lord" (Deut. 6:4).

In Jesus' time, the Jews so reverenced the name of God that they would not say the sacred name *Yahweh* because it was so holy. They took the consonants out of the name Yahweh and the vowels out of the term Adonai, put them together, and formed a new word the *King James* translators spelled "Jehovah." When devout Jews came to the word *Yahweh* they would say *Adonai*, so they would not dishonor God's real name by saying it. When Jewish scholars copied the Scriptures, they selected a new pen with which to write God's name so they would not dishonor God by writing His name with a pen that had been used to write other words. After using the new pen to write God's name, they broke it so it could never be used again.

Many of these same Jews who were so reverent toward God's name, however, blasphemed Him by their self-serving legalism. They outwardly conformed to the law, but their hearts did not worship God. When Jesus taught us to pray "Hallowed be Thy name," He was telling us to make the presence of God real in our hearts.

When you pray "Hallowed be Thy name," you are placing God on the throne of your heart.

When you begin your prayers "Hallowed be Thy name," you are not rushing into God's presence to demand something, nor are you concerned about your sins, or about your ability to pray. You come into His presence recognizing who God is and what He can do for you.

When you pray "Hallowed be Thy name," you are not making a deal with God or placing conditions on Him for answers to prayer. Too many people say, "God, if I stop a sin, will you answer my prayer?" Or they pray, "God, I will do something good for You (like going to church or giving money) if You'll answer my prayer." Some people think God will do what they ask if they pray a long time...like one hour...or one day. All these motivations are wrong. Your prayer is a platform to magnify God. When you pray the Lord's Prayer, you put His glory on display in your life.

When you pray "Hallowed be Thy name," recognize God's names

in the Lord's Prayer. He is your Father, which means He is close to you and intimate. He is also your King, however, the powerful Creator and Ruler of the Universe, the One who has established the laws of nature and has decreed future events by eternal fiat.

So in the Lord's Prayer you enter the family room of a Father-God who is concerned about your hurts and needs. You also enter reverently and fearfully into the throne room of a God-King who demands obedience and reverence.

GOD'S NAME IS HOLY

"Hallowed" is an old word that has little meaning to people today. When people think of hallowed they think of morbid sanctuaries...or mournful music...or halos on saints...or the altar inside the church where they are not supposed to go.

To pray with the heart, we need to examine the meaning of the word "hallowed." It comes from the Greek word *hagios*, which is also the word for "holy." When you pray "Hallowed be Thy name," you are saying, "Let Your name be holy on earth as it is holy in heaven."

A related verb, *hagiadzo*, means "to make holy" or "to separate." This means that God is separate from anything on earth that is worldly, profane or sinful. God is holy. Our prayer should be like the angels who cry, "Holy, holy, holy, is the Lord of hosts: the whole earth is full of his glory" (Isa. 6:3).

Therefore, when you pray "Hallowed be Thy name," you are setting God apart in your thinking and feeling. You are treating Him with all the respect that is due His character.

When you hallow the name of God, you are giving Him the honor He deserves. Worship is giving to God the *worthship* that is due Him.

To understand how God's name can be glorified, notice the prayer of Moses. "Show me thy glory," Moses prayed in Exodus 33:18. He was praying on top of Mount Sinai when the power of God came down in the Shekinah glory cloud. Already, Moses had seen more of God's glory than had any other man, yet he asks, "Show me thy glory." How did God do this?

"The Lord descended in the cloud, and stood with him there, and proclaimed the name of the Lord" (34:5). What is the name God proclaimed? "And the Lord passed by before him, and proclaimed, The Lord, The Lord God, merciful and gracious, longsuffering, and abundant in goodness and truth, keeping mercy for thousands, forgiving iniquity and transgression and sin" (v. 6,7).

God told Moses that His name was the composite of all His attributes. That is, God's name is who He is.

So when you pray "Hallowed be Thy name," you are recognizing all of God's attributes; you are recognizing who He is. All that God is, is embodied in His name. When you hallow His name, you lift up His Person.

GOD WANTS US TO PRAISE HIM

Teaching His followers that God wants truehearted worshipers, Jesus said, "The Father seeketh such to worship him" (John 4:23). In this statement, He was suggesting how we should begin our prayers. We begin with "Hallowed be Thy name" because God desires that we praise Him. This is what He has asked us to do.

When you pray, therefore, remember that God's glory is greater than your problems...greater than your needs...greater than your fears...greater than anything you want to do for Him. Begin your prayers with "Hallowed be Thy name" because the most important thing in prayer is that God's name be magnified and exalted.

What does God get out of your prayers? When we begin praying, we become God conscious. Ask yourself, What does God need from me?

Because God can perform miracles, He doesn't need our help....
Because He is all-knowing, He doesn't need our advice....
Because He is all-powerful, He doesn't need our help....
Because He is rich, He doesn't need our money....
Because He is God, He wants our worship.

Think of the Lord's Prayer as *communion*. It is talking with God. How would ordinary citizens feel if they could talk to the president of the United States? Most would be overwhelmed with the moment. We would be intimidated because he is so powerful and we are so ordinary.

We might also be intimidated when we enter God's presence. If we enter on His conditions, and on His invitation, however, we begin praying "Hallowed be Thy name"—and He graciously accepts us in His presence.

He invites you to come. Jesus said, "Come unto me" (Matt. 11:28).

"The Spirit and the bride say, Come....let him that is athirst come" (Rev. 22:17).

"The Father seeketh such to worship him" (John 4:23).

I CAN PRAISE GOD'S NAME WITH THE LORD'S PRAYER

Americans are very eager to treat God in a friendly way because we are friendly people. Many of our American churches have lost the sense of holiness and reverence by our informal approach to God. We stick out our hand and ask God, "How ya doing?" Or we yell across the room, "Good morning, Lord."

Informality has its place because God is family. But Jesus told us to begin, "Hallowed [holy] be Thy name."

The purpose of the Lord's Prayer is to set God in His rightful place in our lives. It is not primarily about getting things.

It is not primarily about confronting sins. It is about putting God on the throne of our lives on earth, as He sits upon His throne in heaven.

When you pray "Hallowed be Thy name," you are giving God a platform in your life from which He can manifest His glory. When you honestly make this petition, you focus your mind on the Person of God, and keep it there until you understand the greatness of who God is and what He can do for you.

You don't pray the Lord's Prayer to impress God with your spirituality or with your ability to pray. First, like booting up a computer screen, display God to your mind, and then worship Him.

In the introduction, I told of trying to pray for one hour, and thinking I had prayed for a couple of hours when I had actually prayed only 17 minutes. Now I can pray longer because it is not a "sales pitch" to the Almighty. I talk to God. I worship Him for Himself. Because God is so big and has so many attributes, it takes a long time to praise Him for all that He is to me.

GOD WILL NOT FORCE
ANYONE TO PRAISE HIS NAME

The Lord's Prayer teaches the sovereignty of God the King, but it also teaches that people have a free will. Adam could choose to eat of the forbidden fruit...David could choose adultery...Abraham could choose to lie...Peter could choose to deny...and Judas could choose to betray...and they all chose wrong.

Worship is a choice.

The Psalms command God's people to "Worship the Lord in the beauty of holiness" (96:9).

The Psalms command the unsaved, "Make a joyful noise unto the Lord, all ye lands" (100:1).

The command is to worship God, but many do not do it. Some are ignorant, although their inner hearts know God. Some are rebellious because of sin. Some are too busy because of the cares of this world. Some have forgotten because other things crowd out Jesus.

The Lord is waiting on the phone, but we must pick up the receiver to talk to Him. Begin praying this day, "Hallowed be Thy name." Pray it several times this day.

WORSHIP IS A TWO-WAY STREET

Praise is a two-way street. Your needs are met when you glorify the Father. When you go to God with your worship, He comes to help you with your problems.

When you need understanding...praise your Father through the perfect Person of Jesus Christ. Say, "Our Father," and your Father, who gave life to you, will understand you.

When you feel lonely...praise your Father through Jesus Christ our intercessor. Say, "Our Father," and your Father, who knows your nature, will be your helper and Your friend.

When you have failed...praise your Father through the blood of Jesus Christ. Say, "Our Father," and your Father, who knows your failure even before you tell Him, will forgive you and encourage you in doing the right thing.

God reaches down to touch you as you reach up to touch Him.

PRAYER CHECKLIST

Hallowed be Thy name *List what you want to praise God for.*	**How are you doing? (check one)**		
	Lousy	*Average*	*Great*
1.			
2.			
3.			
4.			
5.			
6.			
7.			

JOURNALING

If you are serious about growing as a believer, keep a record of how you worship God. Evaluate yourself. Compare one week with a previous seven-day period. Are you growing in your understanding of God or in your worship of God? Use the following questions to guide your journaling.

1. What words are you using to worship God? (i.e., praise, magnify, hallowed, exalt, lift up, revive, etc.).
2. What are the names of God you use to worship Him?
3. Are you using hymns to worship God? Which hymns? What are you learning from the hymns?
4. Are you growing in your understanding of worship? How?
5. How are you changing your worship expression?

THREE-STEP BIBLE STUDY
THY NAME BE HALLOWED

This Bible study shows you why God's name is special and how you can make it "hallowed" in your life. Step 1—Read the questions to get you thinking about God's name. Step 2—Analyze the verses with each question to see what the Bible says about the question. Step 3—Write your answers in the space provided.

1. God's name stands for His Person. What should be your response to God's name?

> "Blessed be the name of the Lord from this time forth and for evermore."—Psalm 113:2

_____
_____
_____
_____

2. How serious is God about our misuse of His name?

> "Thou shalt not take the name of the Lord thy God in vain; for the Lord will not hold him guiltless that taketh his name in vain."—Exodus 20:7

_____
_____
_____
_____

3. How should all people respond to God's name?

> "Hear thou in heaven thy dwelling place, and do according to all that the stranger calleth to thee for: that all people of the earth may know thy name, to fear thee, as do thy people Israel; and that they may know that this house [Solomon's Temple], which I have builded, is called by thy name."—1 Kings 8:43

_____
_____
_____
_____

4. What happens among non-Christians when God's
   name is glorified?

> "That your name will be great forever. Then men will say,
> 'The Lord Almighty, the God over Israel, is Israel's God.'"
> —1 Chronicles 17:24 (NIV)

_____
_____
_____
_____

5. What should be the Christian's response to God's
   name?

> "Stand up and bless the Lord your God forever and ever!
> Blessed be Your glorious name, which is exalted above all
> blessing and praise!"—Nehemiah 9:5 (NKJV)

_____
_____
_____
_____

6. What can be said for God's name, and what is our
   attitude?

> "Holy and reverend is his name."—Psalm 111:9
> "And one [Seraphim] cried unto another, and said, Holy,
> holy, holy, is the Lord of hosts: the whole earth is full of
> his glory"—Isaiah 6:3

_____
_____

---

7. When we "hallow" God's name, we worship His Person. How does God want us to treat His name?

> "The hour cometh, and now is, when the true worshippers shall worship the Father in spirit and in truth: for the Father seeketh such to worship him. God is a Spirit: and they that worship him must worship him in spirit and in truth."—John 4:23,24

The Lord's Prayer Is...

Not About Posture
God's people prayed standing, kneeling, lying, with folded hands, uplifted hands, bowed heads, lifted heads, eyes closed, eyes open, etc. The Lord's Prayer is about an open heart to God.

Not About a Place
God's people prayed on a mountain, in a field, in a boat, in a house, in the Temple, in battle, doing their jobs, walking into their homes, walking out of their homes, etc. The Lord's Prayer is to be prayed anywhere.

Not About a Time
God's people prayed in the morning, noon, evening and at night upon their beds; before meals, before harvest, during work, in worship. The Lord's Prayer is for any time of the day, any time in your physical growth and any time in your spiritual growth.

Everyone's Prayer
The Lord's Prayer should be prayed by all people, at all times, in all circumstances, in all places, in all weather, in all houses, in all the outdoors, in all work, in all play, in all relationships, in all trouble, in all places of happiness...because the Lord's Prayer is the all-everything prayer.

— 4 —

THE SECOND
PETITION:
THY KINGDOM COME

Learning Kingdom Principles

The small son was playing with his french fries, dipping the end of one in the ketchup, then waving it like a baton. His father was enjoying the moment. Mother had gone to a seminar, so for lunch the father took out his son and bought him a hamburger and french fries. The young boy was more interested in playing with the french fries than eating them, though.

"Eat your french fries..." the father coaxed.

The son continued to wave his "french-fry baton," and the band played on. The father looked at his watch, but he did not have anywhere he had to be. It was his habit to hurry about everything. After lunch, they were just going back home.

Then almost by instinct, the father reached over and did something most fathers have done. He took one french fry out of his son's package.

"No!" the son said sharply, and slapped the fathers hand. Then, raising his voice, he repeated, "No!" Apparently no one saw the little boy slap at his father's hand. No one heard what the little boy said.

The stunned father sat surveying the situation, though saying nothing. *Who does he think he is?* he thought. *He's my son...I bought these french fries, and I should be able to eat the fries that he won't eat!*

That was not the case, though. The little boy had already gone back to leading his make-believe band as though he had forgotten the situation. The father, however, had not forgotten what happened. He thought to himself, *I could get mad and never buy him another french fry in his life.*

The father was not mad at his son, though; he was more surprised than anything. He was not the type to get even. If anything, he was a mild kind of guy. He continued to think. *I could bury him in french fries and smother him in ketchup, I love him so much.*

The father sat in the plastic chair, watching his son dip another fry in ketchup, and lead the band. The little guy had no idea of the thoughts going through his father's mind.

We are like little children playing at life. Our heavenly Father reaches over to take one of our french fries–say in the form of wanting a couple of hours of worship on Sunday, or asking that we support His Church with our money.

Too often we slap God's hand, telling Him,

"No! Keep Your hand out of my life."

God does not want to take all our french fries from us. He wants just a taste. Like a selfish child, however, we say, "No!"

The question of the little boy and his father is a question about our heavenly Father and His children:

Who owns your french fries?

When we pray "Thy kingdom come," we recognize that God is the ruler of our lives. We recognize that God owns our french fries.

The second petition, "Thy kingdom come," teaches us five main truths.

FIVE ESSENTIAL FACTS ABOUT GOD'S KINGDOM

1. God is our Ruler-King
2. God has a kingdom He rules
3. God's kingdom does not exist fully in the present
4. God's kingdom *can* come in the here and now
5. The Lord's Prayer can help bring in God's kingdom

When you bow to pray the Lord's Prayer, you first pray, "Our Father who art in heaven." You recognize that God is your Father who is close and intimate, who cares for you.

In the second petition, you pray, "Thy kingdom come." You recognize God as the lofty One who rules from the throne of heaven.

In the third petition you pray, "Thy will be done." You recognize God as your King who has a plan for your life. As a King, God wants to rule your life with His principles and for His purpose.

GOD IS OUR RULER-KING

What do people expect from a king? This is a difficult thought for people who live in a democracy. In the United States we don't look to a king, because we believe in the vote of the people. The Constitution of the United States begins, "We the People." People in a democracy rule themselves.

There are three branches of American government, or three sources of power. These are identified as the three functions of government.

First, the legislative branch (Congress) determines rules by which we live.

Second, the judicial branch (courts and judges) interpret and apply our laws to specific cases.

Third, the executive branch (the president) administers government for us.

Christians also live under God, who is King. David said, "Thou art my King, O God" (Ps. 44:4). God rules His kingdom just as the American democracy is ruled by the three branches of government.

First, God determines the rules of His kingdom in heaven, as well as on earth.

Second, He judges rule breakers and rewards those who keep his law.

Finally, God is the Executive Administrator of His kingdom.

GOD HAS A KINGDOM HE RULES

When you pray "Thy kingdom come," first you are inviting God to rule in your heart by His principles. That makes His kingdom internal and personal. He is your personal King and you are His subject. You are praying, "Thy kingdom rule in my heart, as Thy kingdom is ruled in heaven." Obviously, because we are imperfect people, God's rule is not perfect. The standard is always there, however. We should allow God to rule us today, as He will rule us after we enter heaven.

HOW GOD RULES IN HEAVEN

1. Right purpose
2. Right motive
3. Right timing
4. Right decisions
5. Right sensitivity
6. Right respect
7. Right according to His standards

The rule of God on earth is called the kingdom of God. Not everyone is a member of God's kingdom. A person must join the Kingdom and pledge allegiance to the King. People enter the Kingdom when they are born again. Jesus said, "Except a man be born again, he cannot see the kingdom of God" (John 3:3). You must have a spiritual birth to enter into His kingdom. Receiving Jesus as your Savior is the same as believing in Him. "As many as received Him [Christ], to them He gave the right to become children of God" (1:12, *NKJV*).

After we enter the kingdom, we must please God, who is our King. "But seek ye first the kingdom of God, and his righteousness; and all these things [earthly necessities] shall be added unto you" (Matt. 6:33).

When you pray "Thy kingdom come," you are also asking for the spread of the gospel to those who do not belong to Christ. "Thy kingdom come" is a prayer for soul winning and evangelism. You are praying for the Kingdom to be expanded into the lives of people who will become rightly related to the King. As you think of unsaved friends and relatives, you are praying for their salvation every time you ask, "Thy kingdom come."

There is a corporate sense of expanding God's kingdom. You can pray for the evangelization of a neighborhood in which your church is attempting to establish a new mission church. You may not actually know anyone in that neighborhood. When you pray "Thy kingdom come," though, you are asking for that new church to be effective.

When you pray "Thy kingdom come," you are asking for foreign missionaries who will preach the gospel of Jesus Christ to those who have never heard it. You are asking for God's kingdom to come in "foreign mission fields." The songwriter, Isaac Watts, described this action:

> Jesus shall reign where-e'er the sun
> Does His successive journeys run;
> His kingdom spread from shore to shore,
> Till moons shall wax and wane no more.
> —Isaac Watts (1674-1748)

There is another aspect of praying "Thy kingdom come." You are asking for the return of Jesus to establish His kingdom on this earth. This prayer recognizes that God's kingdom is not presently ruling on earth. When you pray "Thy kingdom come," you are asking for the second coming of Jesus to this earth.

If you pray "Thy kingdom come," God will give you a crown:

> Henceforth there is laid up for me a crown of righteousness, which the Lord, the righteous judge, shall give me at that day:....unto all them also that love his appearing (2 Tim. 4:8).

You are expressing love for God's coming kingdom when you ask for it to come. The last prayer in the Bible is an echo of this petition in the Lord's Prayer: "Even so, come, Lord Jesus" (Rev. 22:20).

When the King comes, all earthly kings will no longer rule. God will be King-Ruler. "The kingdoms of this world are become the kingdoms of our Lord, and of his Christ; and he shall reign for ever and ever" (Rev. 11:15).

All persecution will cease, for the "pharaohs" who persecuted God's people will be gone. All death will cease, for tyrants such as King Sennacherib, who destroyed the Northern Kingdom of Israel, will be gone. All hatred and racial prejudice, like that of King Nebuchadnezzar of Babylon against Israel, will cease. All criticism and attacks on the Church, like that of King Herod who tried to kill the baby Jesus, will be gone.

CHAPTER FOUR

GOD'S KINGDOM DOES NOT EXIST FULLY IN THE PRESENT

You admit that God's kingdom is not here in its fullness when you pray, "Thy kingdom come." God wants to rule His earth, but people reject Him, as they have always done.

God called His people in the Old Testament to follow Him. He delivered them from slavery out of Egypt. They walked through the Red Sea on dry land, and for 40 years in the wilderness, God took care of His people. He fed them manna and gave them water from the rock to drink. He promised them the land of Canaan and gave it to them.

Once in the Promised Land, God wanted to be their King. His people, however, cried out, "Make us a king to judge us like all the nations" (1 Sam. 8:5). God interpreted their request as unbelief and rebellion: "They have rejected me, that I should not reign over them" (1 Sam. 8:7).

God sent them another King. It was His Son, who was born in a manger in Bethlehem. Wise men from the east asked, "Where is he that is born King of the Jews? for we have seen his star in the east, and are come to worship him" (Matt. 2:2). The Jewish King Herod, however, tried to kill the baby King.

Jesus came preaching, "The kingdom of heaven is at hand" (4:17), but He was rejected by the Jews. Jesus was tried before a Roman judge. The Jews cried out, "Away with him,...crucify him....We have no king but Caesar" (John 19:15).

They crowned their King with thorns, and crucified Him. Sovereignly, God guided Pilate to write the reason for His execution on the cross: "JESUS OF NAZARETH THE KING OF THE JEWS" (v. 19).

Today Jesus does not have an outward kingdom. He does not have an earthly kingdom. He rules in the hearts of those who accept Him and yield themselves to Him. Paul points to Him as such a Ruler: "Now unto the King eternal, immortal, invisible, the only wise God, be honour and glory for ever and ever. Amen" (1 Tim. 1:17).

CHARACTERISTICS OF THE KINGDOM TODAY

1. Inward rule
2. Invisible rule
3. Rule of love
4. Rule by self-discipline
5. Rule of grace

GOD'S KINGDOM *CAN* COME IN THE HERE AND NOW

When you pray "Thy kingdom come," you are asking for something that is not yet here to come into existence. You are asking for God's kingdom to manifest itself through your life.

People pray for the Kingdom to come for many reasons. Some, when facing a painful death by cancer, pray, "Thy kingdom come." They can't take any more pain. They want a quick and painless death.

Some face pressures at the job. They are miserable...not enough money...not enough time...not enough energy to get them through the day. They pray "Thy kingdom come" because they want God's peace and happiness.

Some are frustrated and defeated. They have gone through bankruptcy...they have gone through more than one divorce...their kids have not turned out right...they have failed everyone. They pray "Thy kingdom come" because they want a second start—they want a "born-again" opportunity to try all over again. They wonder if God is the One who will give them that second chance.

Some are addicts...they are helpless slaves to drugs or alcohol...they are sexual addicts. These are the people that can't say no to a habit and they can't say yes to God. Like Paul, they weep, "For the good that I would I do not: but the evil which I would not, that I do" (Rom. 7:19). They pray "Thy kingdom come," wanting God to enter their lives to give them the ability to do right.

Then there are some who want God's rule in their lives. They have never been in jail and they are not addicts to anything. They do not have a deadly disease, nor is there an emergency in their lives. They pray "Thy kingdom come" because they love God and want the principles of Jesus to rule in their lives. They have not been disobedient; they just want to love God more.

There are some who walk with Christ, who slip into a Bible class carrying the Word of God under their arms. They open its pages to the lesson and pray, "Thy kingdom come in my life." They are asking for God to teach them how to live by His principles. They want His kingdom to come into their lives in a better way in the coming week—better than the previous week.

Anyone can sign up for the Kingdom. Jesus said, "If anyone wants to follow me, they should stop living for themselves and follow My principles daily" (Luke 9:23, author's paraphrase). The businessman can stop dedicating his life to money and follow Christ. Then, applying biblical principles of vocation, he will be a better businessman.

The mother who selfishly lives for her family can follow Christ. Then, having obtained a higher standard of Christ's love, she will be a better mother.

The politician who seeks fame and position can follow Christ. Then, serving in the kingdom of God, he can serve in political office better than ever.

Children can pray "Thy kingdom come in my life," for Jesus said, "Permit the little children to come to me" (Matt. 19:14, author's translation).

Teenagers can pray "Thy kingdom come in my life" because John said, "I have written unto you, young men, because ye are strong, and the word of God abideth in you" (1 John 2:14).

Senior citizens can pray "Thy kingdom come in my life" because Paul writes about the "aged men" (Titus 2:2) and "aged women" (v. 3).

THE LORD'S PRAYER CAN HELP BRING IN GOD'S KINGDOM

Implied in the Lord's Prayer is that you can make a difference. If you pray "Thy kingdom come," God can send His kingdom to be manifested on earth, as it is manifested in heaven. Jesus also seems to imply that if we *don't* pray "Thy kingdom come," then it probably won't come. The Kingdom coming to earth is, in part, a choice.

Your choice.

You can help bring in God's kingdom. Of course, God will bring in the kingdom in its fullness by Himself, when He wants to do it. The eternal tension between God's work and people's responsibility is seen in the Lord's Prayer. God is sovereign; He can and will bring His kingdom to earth without us. He has, however, commanded us to pray "Thy kingdom come" to allow us to express our choice in the matter.

God sometimes allows people to mess up His work. He chose Joseph to do His work, but Joseph's brothers tried to kill him, then sold him as a slave so that he ended up in Egypt. God, however, worked it out for Joseph to save his brothers and his family (see Gen. 45—46).

We were predestined before the foundations of the earth (see Eph. 1:5), and the blood of Christ was shed for our sins in eternity past (see 1 Pet. 1:18-20). Yet we must repent and receive Christ, and we are warned that wrong decisions will lead to God's judgment (see Heb. 2:1-4).

Your choice is crucial.

When you pray "Thy kingdom come," you indicate that you have decided to live for God...you have chosen to live by His principles...you have decided to glorify God in your life. Life is a choice, and you have chosen the Kingdom.

When you pray "Thy kingdom come," you usually don't bring it in all at once. The prayer is like educating a child—it usually takes 12 years of school to obtain a high school diploma. It may take God 12 years to bring His kingdom principles into your life because you need to learn a lot of lessons for God's kingdom to come into your life.

Still, when you pray "Thy kingdom come," you plant a seed. Although the Kingdom is not manifest in your life immediately, it begins to take root like a newly planted seed. It may not produce fruit overnight. Jesus recognized the slow but sure plan for growth: "First the blade, then the ear, after that the full corn in the ear" (Mark 4:28). It takes time for Kingdom principles to produce fruit in your life.

PRAYER CHECKLIST

Thy kingdom come *List how you want God to rule your life.*	How are you doing? (check one)		
	Lousy	*Average*	*Great*
1.			
2.			
3.			
4.			
5.			
6.			
7.			

JOURNALING

Each day you will pray for God's kingdom to come into your life. Make a list of ways you want this to be accomplished. As you pray for these specifics, describe the answer in your journal—both positive answers and things God does not seem to be doing. When you analyze the "non-answers," you may find out why God is not answering your prayers.

God brings His kingdom into your life by teaching you Kingdom principles and helping you live by His standards. Each day write out in complete sentences the new Kingdom principles you are learning. Then apply the Kingdom principles to other areas of your life. Write out how you are applying them.

1. What Kingdom principles are you learning?
2. In what areas of your life are you applying them?
3. How well are you doing in applying them?
4. What is God teaching you as you pray "Thy kingdom come"?

THREE-STEP BIBLE STUDY

FINDING KINGDOM PRINCIPLES FOR LIVING

The following three-step Bible study is designed to help you apply Kingdom principles to your life. When you pray "Thy kingdom come," for what are you asking?

1. A king has many responsibilities to his followers. What obligations does God have to us?

> "Hearken unto the voice of my cry, my King, and my God: for unto thee will I pray."—Psalm 5:2

_____

_____

2. What is one of your obligations to our King-God?

"So shall the king greatly desire thy beauty: for he is thy Lord; and worship thou him."—Psalm 45:11

_____

_____

_____

_____

3. How can you enter God's kingdom and become His follower?

"Jesus answered and said unto him, Verily, verily, I say unto thee, Except a man be born again, he cannot see the kingdom of God."—John 3:3

_____

_____

_____

4. What is your obligation as a follower of the King?

"But seek ye first the kingdom of God, and his righteousness; and all these things shall be added unto you."
—Matthew 6:33

_____

_____

_____

5. Is God's kingdom physical, and do you live in a physical kingdom? Why or why not?

"Jesus answered, My kingdom is not of this world: if my kingdom were of this world, then would my servant fight, that I should not be delivered to the Jews: but now is my kingdom not from hence."—John 18:36

_____
_____
_____

6. If you don't live in a physical kingdom, what rules does the kingdom of God have over you?

"For the kingdom of God is not meat and drink; but righteousness, and peace, and joy in the Holy Ghost."
—Romans 14:17

_____
_____
_____

7. Every kingdom has punishment for breaking its laws. What are the laws of God's kingdom, and how will He punish the lawbreakers?

"Now the works of the flesh are manifest, which are these; Adultery, fornication, uncleanness, lasciviousness, idolatry, witchcraft, hatred, variance, emulations, wrath, strife, seditions, heresies, envyings, murders, drunkenness, revellings, and such like: of the which I tell you before, as I have also told you in time past, that they which do such things shall not inherit the kingdom of God."—Galatians 5:19-21

_____
_____
_____

8. What are the rewards of God's kingdom?

> "Giving thanks unto the Father, which hath made us meet to be partakers of the inheritance of the saints in light: who hath delivered us from the power of darkness, and hath translated us into the kingdom of his dear Son: in whom we have redemption through his blood, even the forgiveness of sins."—Colossians 1:12-14

_____
_____
_____
_____

9. When shall God's spiritual rule in our hearts become a physical kingdom?

> "And the seventh angel sounded [the trumpet]; and there were great voices in heaven, saying, The kingdoms of this world are become the kingdoms of our Lord, and of his Christ; and he shall reign for ever and ever."—Revelation 11:15

_____
_____
_____
_____

10. What shall be your response when God's kingdom is manifested physically?

> "Wherefore God also hath highly exalted him, and given him a name which is above every name: that at the name of Jesus every knee should bow, of things in heaven, and things in earth, and things under the earth; and that every tongue should confess that Jesus Christ is Lord, to the glory of God the Father."—Philippians 2:9-11

The Lord's Prayer:
The All-Inclusive Prayer

It is to be prayed...

> By all believers,
> Of all ages,
> In all centuries,
> At all times,
> In all churches,
> At all levels of maturity,
> In all circumstances,
> With all your heart.

THE THIRD PETITION:
THY WILL BE DONE

Submitting to God's Plan for Your Life

The dining-room floor was covered with a coat of winter dirt, not to mention some leaves and dust bunnies in the corner. Mopping was difficult because the porous concrete soaked up the soapy water from my mop. The old cotton mop left strings of white lint on the floor.

About midnight, my buddies left for bed, leaving me to finish cleaning the large dining room by myself. Ben Lippen Camp, Asheville, North Carolina, had been closed for the winter and I was one of three college boys hired to prepare everything for summer campers. My buddies laughed at me for being a workaholic.

"Finish it for us," they said. "We'll see you in the morning."

I was whistling while I worked.

Then I saw it, right in the middle of the room. It was tacked to a post. It was a dark blue poster printed in silver letters. I read it and stopped dead in my tracks. Leaning on the mop handle, I was fascinated with the message because it answered the biggest question in my thinking at the time. I did not know what to do with my life; and the dark blue sign read,

God Has A Plan For Your Life

God's plan is for me to finish mopping this floor, I thought.
Then I wondered what else God wanted me to do.
"Hmm..." I said, to no one in particular.
The thought of God's plan for my life intrigued me. So I asked myself, *What does God want me to do when I finish mopping the floor?*
"Hmm...."
God wants me to do a good job by picking up the white lint, I thought.
"Hmm...."
God wants me to get a good night's sleep so I can work hard tomorrow!
"Hmm...."
God wants me to be a good camp counselor this summer.
"Hmm...."
God wants me to get a good education so I can serve Him better.
I stood in front of this blue and silver poster for almost half an hour. I thought of all the things God wanted me to do. Then I thought of all the things I had not done; and that was a discouraging thought.
Next I thought about all the things I had to do. I had to sleep, eat, exercise, learn and go to the bathroom. Because God created people who had to do these things...they must be God's plan for my life.
What about the Ten Commandments? I thought.
I recognized that God's plan involved telling the truth, being sexually pure, not stealing, obeying my parents and not making graven images...whatever that meant. I did not know what a "graven image" was, but given God told me not to have one...you can bet your last dollar I would not make one, or even buy one.
What about my vocation? I thought.
Because God had a plan for my life, I yielded my future to God

that night. Many people have heard a seminar about this topic, and in response they have gone to a church altar to pray. In my case, however, my church altar was the handle of a mop. I bowed my head over the end of that mop and yielded my life to God there in the dining hall at Ben Lippen Camp, sometime after midnight.

My mind often drifts back to that silver and blue poster. I think about the late-night encounter that gave direction to my life. I now wish I had taken the poster down to keep it on my desk. I would like to have it to remind me constantly of my obligation to God's purpose for my life. But I don't have the poster.

Sometime during the next two weeks, someone threw away the blue sign. It was greasy. The silver painting was cracked. The corners were frayed. Although the sign was old and unattractive to youthful campers, the message gripped me just as the Lord's Prayer fascinates me today.

When you pray "Thy will be done," you are not just asking God to guide the economic future of a nation, nor are you asking for a military victory in a war. You are asking for God's will to be done in your life on earth, as His will is done in heaven. This petition of the Lord's Prayer is based on the same premise as that sign in the dining hall: GOD HAS A PLAN FOR YOUR LIFE.

When you pray "Thy will be done," you are admitting five truths about God's will.

FIVE ESSENTIAL FACTS ABOUT GOD'S WILL

1. God has a plan for your personal life
2. Following God's plan is good for you
3. You can find and do God's will now
4. God's plan is not forced on you
5. The Lord's Prayer will help you find God's plan

When you pray "Thy will be done on earth, as it is in heaven," you confess that there is a great difference between the two places. In heaven, angels do not pray about God's will; they just do it. In heaven, God's will is done instantly, not later. In heaven, God's will is done enthusiastically, not halfheartedly. In heaven, God's will is done completely, not partially. In heaven, God's will is done perfectly, not as we do it on earth.

GOD HAS A PLAN FOR YOUR PERSONAL LIFE

When you pray "Thy will be done," realize what you are asking. If you recognize God as your Father, it is like saying, "We'll go on our vacation where You want us to go." You are telling your Father to make plans for you. If you recognize God as your King, when you pray "Thy will be done," you are surrendering your will to your Sovereign.

When you pray "Thy will be done," you should know what you mean by God's will. Otherwise, you do not know what you are getting. The will of God could mean two things.

First, the will of God could mean His overall plan for your life, like a blueprint an architect follows in constructing a building. So you are praying, "Thy long-range blueprint for my life be done." You are asking God to build your life as He might construct a building using His plans.

Second, praying "Thy will be done" means you trust the decision-making ability of God. You are asking God to guide *your* decisions by *His* decision-making ability. In the middle of a battle, the commander will make a series of decisions to deploy troops, move artillery and provide supplies. The commander has an overall plan or strategy. That's the "Big Picture." The commander also makes daily decisions. This is how he guides his troops to victory. So when you pray "Thy will be done," you are asking for God's decisions to be effective in your life based on His ability to see the "big picture"; and you are asking for His guidance in your life for the problems of that day.

WHAT IS GOD'S WILL?

As a *noun*, it is like a blueprint for your life. (The Big Picture.)

As a *verb*, God *will!* He *will* make competent decisions for your life. (Guidance.)

There are several expressions of God's will.

First, there is the *automatic* will of God. These are like the laws by which God runs the universe. These are His strategies, or the laws of nature. God's will is automatically done when you breathe. You don't have to make a decision to take a breath. You automatically breathe because breathing is an expression of human nature. God's plan included a respiration system for each of us, and the creation of air to breathe.

When a pencil rolls off a table, it automatically falls down because of another automatic will of God—the law of gravity.

In addition to such laws of nature, God's automatic will functions in the laws of heaven. God says, "Surely as I have thought, so shall it come to pass; and as I have purposed, so shall it stand" (Isa. 14:24).

Sometimes you don't need to pray "Thy will be done." It will automatically happen. You don't need to pray for water to boil at 212 degrees Fahrenheit. You don't have to pray for water to run down to the sea. "The Lord of hosts hath purposed, and who shall disannul it?" (v. 27).

A second expression of the will of God is called His *desire*. This consists of things He desires to be done, but that are not always done. God wants certain things done that often don't happen. For example, God wants everyone to believe in Him...*everyone*.

"For God sent not his Son into the world to condemn the world; but that the world through him might be saved" (John 3:17). "The Lord is not slack concerning his promise,...not willing that any should perish, but that all should come to repentance" (2 Pet. 3:9). God does not want anyone to reject Him, but people do not always honor His desire.

The shortest verse in the Bible says, "Jesus wept" (John 11:35). Many know that this is the shortest verse, but few ever ask why God's Son cried. Jesus shed tears because of His grief for the sisters of Lazarus who died, and because of other weeping friends. Jesus was also sorrowful when He faced mockery and rejection by an unbelieving crowd. He wanted everyone to receive Him, but they rejected Him. God's will was thwarted.

When you pray "Thy will be done," you are saying that you want to accomplish the desires of God that might not be done.

The third expression of the will of God is what He *commands*. When a mother says, "Clean up your room!" that command is her will, or her desire. When a father says no to a son, that is an expression of the father's will. God commands His children, "Be ye holy; for I am holy" (1 Pet. 1:16). It is God's will that His children obey Him completely every day, in every way. So the children of God must be holy. Those who are not holy disobey God. When you pray "Thy will be done," you are asking for God's help in carrying out His commands. You are asking God to help you become holy in response to His command.

The Bible contains many commands. Some we know about, and some we have never read. To do God's will, we must learn them and do them.

FOLLOWING GOD'S PLAN IS GOOD FOR YOU

Some people think the will of God is like a box of Cracker Jack. Only once in a while do we get the prize. Most of the time we get a handful of ordinary stuff.

Some people think the will of God is like a bag of marbles. It is something He can pull out...shine up...show off...and use in a game to win some more marbles.

Some people think the will of God is like Santa's bag. It is full of candy and toys, but He only comes once a year to good little boys and girls because He knows who is naughty or nice.

Some people think the will of God is a 911 emergency number to use in case of fire or other emergencies.

Other people think the will of God is the red telephone on the president's desk, to be used as a last resort.

The fact is that doing the Lord's will is the appropriate thing to do.

> Be not influenced by this world, but be supernaturally changed by a new way of thinking, so you can do the will of God that is good and appropriate and perfect (Rom. 12:2, author's translation).

God wants you to do His will because it is good...good for you...good for the family...good for God. When a parent wants a child to come home from a date by midnight, that decision was not made to hurt the child. It is good for the child to have "limits" and learn to obey them. It builds character that will help the child later in life. Limits on a child also help parents sleep better and relieves them of worry. When a young person comes home on time, it is good for the whole family. If one is late, it breaks up family harmony and family plans.

Again, the will of God is appropriate for you. He does not ask you to be the center on His basketball team when you are only 5'10" tall. He does not ask you to teach a Bible class when He has given you spiritual gifts of administration and management. As the tattered silver and blue poster in the dining room stated, GOD HAS A PLAN FOR YOUR LIFE.

When you pray "Thy will be done," you are like a little boy who knows he can't do what his father wants without his help. A father wants his child to ride the new bicycle he received at Christmas. In essence, the child tries to do what the father wants done. But the child keeps falling. So the child asks, "Help me...." The child is not asking for the father to ride the bike. He is not asking his father to make him ride the bike. He is asking, "Help me do your will." Then the father steadies and guides and pushes the bike, keeping his son from falling. All the while, the child thinks he is riding the bike. Actually, the father is running alongside his son, helping him do what the father wants.

The petition "Thy will be done" is in the aorist tense in the original language, which means "point" action. When you ask "Thy will be done," you must be willing to do it "right now."

A mother tells a child to come in from play for dinner, but the child continues to play. The mother goes to the door and announces, "I want you to come in the house this very minute." She means instant obedience.

When you pray "Thy will be done," you should have faith to expect God to do His will instantly through your life. Do not expect God to do instantaneously what you are not willing to do, or to allow Him to help you do.

You Can Find and Do God's Will Now

The third petition of the Lord's Prayer is a request that God's will be done in your life. Notice that you are not asking God to do His will or to change His will; and you do not ask God to bless *your* will. You are asking God to help you find and do His will in your life.

Before you become a Christian, *you* sit on the throne of your life. Like a king, you ruled your life and pleased yourself. The issue of salvation is, Who will sit on the throne of your life? Will *you* sit on your heart's throne, or will you let *Christ* be enthroned there? When you become a believer, you let Christ take control of your life. You say with Paul, "For to me to live is Christ..." (Phil. 1:21). Salvation is a picture of our will saying yes to the issue of allowing Christ to sit on the throne of our lives.

Then we must daily pray, "Thy will be done." When we make that prayer daily, it is a conscious decision to let Christ direct our lives. Each day we say yes. This means that the Christian life is one big YES at the beginning, followed by a smaller yes every day.

So each day when you pray "Thy will be done," you are praying at least four things.

FOUR PETITIONS ABOUT GOD'S PLAN FOR YOUR LIFE

1. Help me find Thy plan
2. Help me understand Thy plan
3. Help me submit to Thy plan
4. Help me accomplish Thy plan

When you pray "Thy will be done," you may be asking God to help you find His plan for you in the Bible and to understand it. David understood that the Word of God had some things in it that he did not understand. He prayed, "Open thou mine eyes, that I may behold wondrous things out of thy law" (Ps. 119:18).

When you pray "Thy will be done," it may be a prayer of yielding your will to God's will. The driving instructor can tell her student how to drive a car, show videos about proper driving and even take the student on an instructional driving course to model proper driving techniques. At some point in time, though, the keys are given to the student. The steering wheel is turned over to the student. The control of the car is yielded to the student.

You may know that God has a plan for your life, and understand what it means. You may have listened to Bible lessons about God's plan for your life and even had a mentor explain the practical steps of how God's plan should be lived. There comes a time, though, when you yield your life to God. You let go. He takes over. Then you understand "Thy will be done."

> You don't pray to bend God's will.
> Prayer bends your will to His.

GOD'S PLAN IS NOT FORCED ON YOU

God has a plan for this universe. It is run by His natural laws. God also has a plan for people. They live by the principles of psychology, sociology, nutrition, hygiene and good mental health. Some refuse to live by God's universal laws and suffer consequences...natural results that come directly from breaking known laws.

God has laws about sexual purity, and those who come in contact with AIDS will probably contract AIDS. Some mistakenly say that God punished them, as though God pushed a button in heaven and they were infected. What really happened is they broke certain health laws by contracting AIDS and were infected. God originally initiated the laws of sanitation, but He had nothing personally to do with their getting the disease. They stepped across the health line.

Sometimes you have not done God's will because you did not know what He wanted. Suppose you did not get a raise you expected at work. You get mad. You may not have received your raise because you did not know what the organization expected. Your supervisor says you did not receive the raise because you failed to fill out the proper paperwork. When the supervisor shows you how to fill out the paperwork, you do it; and the raise comes through.

In the same way, when you pray "Thy will be done," you ask God to show you what to do.

> The submission of yourself
> to God is the beginning
> of your prayer life.

Sometimes when you pray "Thy will be done," you are saying that God does not accept the world the way it is. God does not like crime, ignorance and disease. God does not want lying politicians or corrupt businesses. So when you pray "Thy will be done," you are asking God to change the world. Or, you are praying for God to help you change the world according to His plan.

Many Christians see so much corruption about them that they just throw up their hands in despair. Jesus, however, did not react that way. When Jesus saw corrupt money changers in the Temple, He threw them out. In the spirit of "Thy will be done," Jesus cleansed the Temple twice, at the beginning and end of his earthly ministry.

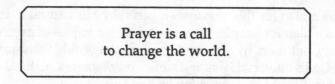

> Prayer is a call
> to change the world.

When you pray "Thy will be done," you also submit your attitude to God. Some people do God's will, but they do it with the wrong attitude. They go to church in submission to God, but they wish they were elsewhere during the service. When bowing in prayer, they desire sinful things. When you pray "Thy will be done," you yield your attitude to God.

Some people drop their money into the offering plate on Sunday, but resentfully think, *I could make a bundle in the stock market with that.* Or they think of the new car or the new suit they need. They may even think, resentfully, *The church should give money to me, instead of my giving to it.* When you pray "Thy will be done," you are asking God to shield you from resentment and to overcome it by a greater trust in Him. When you pray "Thy will be done," you yield your money to God.

Some resent giving time to God. While sitting in church they think, *I could be on the golf course.* Others rationalize, *I work hard to provide for my family. I don't like giving up Sunday family time to attend church.* When you pray "Thy will be done," you confront any resentment about giving your time to God.

Some also have the problem of inward rebellion. They know they must do God's will, but they only surrender outwardly. They think, *I can't beat God, so I might as well surrender.*

A little kindergarten boy kept standing up in class, even though the teacher asked him to sit down. She pressured him, "Everyone else is sitting down. Can't you sit down?" When the boy continued to stand, a teacher helper put her hand on the little boy's shoulder and made him sit down.

In desperation he blurted out, "I may be sitting on the outside, but I'm standing on the inside!"

Some have outwardly submitted to God's will, but inwardly they stubbornly stand up to God. When they pray "Thy will be done," they must inwardly surrender to God's will as well as outwardly do it.

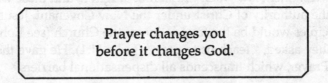

> Prayer changes you
> before it changes God.

Some have an attitude of passive resignation. Like a fatalist, they believe that God causes every problem. Their philosophy is, "Whatever will be...will be." These fatalists don't eagerly pray, "Thy will be done." Nor are these people happy with God's will. They are like a couple who has been married for more than 40 years. The wife jabbers constantly, and the husband sulks in silence. She continues to babble and he has given up trying to change her. He has surrendered.

When you pray "Thy will be done," you are not passively surrendering to God's will just because you can't do anything about it. You actively submit to His plan with joyful anticipation about doing it.

> Prayer is a personal discipline
> that transforms us
> into dedicated disciples.

Some people have theological problems with the Lord's Prayer. They believe God's will only involves what happens in heaven, and not what happens to us on earth. They believe God's will only applied to what happened in Bible times, and not today. If this kind of theology has limited your prayer life, then you have bad theology. When you pray "Thy will be done on earth as it is in heaven," you are asking for: God's intervention...here...now...personally...for you.

Others who believe bad theology teach that the Lord's Prayer is only for those under the Old Testament law or for a future theocratic kingdom. They are applying the Lord's Prayer to the Jewish dispensation. They claim that Jesus taught this prayer before He died, making this an Old Testament prayer. The history of the Christian Church teaches that the Lord's Prayer is for the Church. It is for today...it is for those who live in the United States...it is for anyone in the world today.

The Lord's Prayer is for all believers, including the disciples under the Old Testament law when Christ first taught it, and those who live under the authority of Christ under the New Covenant. Jesus knew His disciples would be the foundation of the Church (see Eph. 2:20). When they asked, "Teach us to pray" (Luke 11:1), He gave them the Lord's Prayer, which transcends all dispensational barriers.

THE LORD'S PRAYER WILL HELP YOU FIND GOD'S PLAN

You can find God's plan for your life if you will pray daily "Thy will be done"...not just repeating the words, but seeking God's will with all your heart. Jesus told us, "Seek ye first the kingdom of God" (Matt. 6:33).

To some, the plan of God comes slowly and gradually, like the dawning of a new day. The sun does not burst on the scene suddenly. There is a faint trace of light to drive away the shadows long before you are able to read the morning newspaper by the faint light in the east. So God's plan comes slowly to those who are in the bondage of sin. As they continue praying daily "Thy will be done," however, God leads them into His plan for their lives.

To others, the plan of God is like turning on the light in a dark room. Young people have gone to church without a clue or direction for their lives. In one missionary conference, though, their lives may become focused. They walk out of the meeting headed for the mission field. They know God has called them that evening, and they obey.

The Lord's Prayer teaches us not to rush into God's presence like children...babbling about our problems...or anticipating a gift. We are taught to come into God's presence to glorify Him...to acknowledge His agenda...to seek His will. The Lord's Prayer teaches us to pray "Thy will be done," and to let God reveal His plan in our lives.

PRAYER CHECKLIST			
Thy kingdom come *List how you want God to rule your life.*	**How are you doing? (check one)**		
	Lousy	*Average*	*Great*
1.			
2.			
3.			
4.			
5.			
6.			
7.			

JOURNALING

If you are serious about finding and doing God's will, you ought to keep a record of how you are doing. Just as a good track record will give direction for the future, so you will better understand God's will when you look back on your present struggles to find God's plan for your life. Answer some of the following questions each day.

1. What principles are you discovering that help you find God's plan for your life?
2. What do you know for sure that God wants you to do?
3. What do you know for sure that God *does not* want you to do? How do you know this?
4. How is your life changing because you are discovering God's plan for your life?

THREE-STEP BIBLE STUDY
HOW TO FIND GOD'S WILL

The following Bible study is designed to help you pray "Thy will be done" in a way that helps you adopt God's will in your life. Step 1—Read the question and try to answer it. Step 2—Read the Bible verse printed in the box, and try to determine how it answers the question. Step 3—Write the answer in the space provided.

1. Because God's will sometimes seems knowable, what is your response?

> "The meek will he guide in judgment: and the meek will he teach his way."—Psalm 25:9
> "Be ye not unwise, but understanding what the will of the Lord is."—Ephesians 5:17

_____

_____

_____

2. What is God's will for you concerning this world?

> "Grace be to you and peace from God the Father, and from our Lord Jesus Christ, who gave himself for our sins, that he might deliver us from this present evil world, according to the will of God and our Father."—Galatians 1:3,4

_____

_____

_____

3. What is the will of God for your physical life?

> "I beseech you therefore, brethren, by the mercies of God, that ye present your bodies a living sacrifice, holy, acceptable unto God, which is your reasonable service. And be not conformed to this world: but be ye transformed by the renewing of your mind, that ye may prove what is that good, and acceptable, and perfect, will of God."—Romans 12:1,2

4. God's will is that you overcome temptation (see 1 Cor. 10:13), and overcome the world (see 1 John 5:4). What does He promise you if you are victorious?

> "And the world passeth away, and the lust thereof: but he that doeth the will of God abideth for ever."—1 John 2:17

5. How can you find the will of God for your life?

> "If anyone wants to know God's will, that person should find out what God wants him to know."—John 7:17 (author's translation)

6. Where can you find the will of God?

> "Of his own will begat he us with the word of truth, that we should be a kind of firstfruits of his creatures."
> —James 1:18

_____

_____

_____

_____

7. When you are not sure of your actions, what should be your response?

> "Then Paul answered, What mean ye to weep and to break mine heart? for I am ready not to be bound only, but also to die at Jerusalem for the name of the Lord Jesus. And when he would not be persuaded, we ceased, saying, The will of the Lord be done."—Acts 21:13,14

_____

_____

_____

_____

8. Paul said he hoped to go to Rome by the will of God (Rom. 1:10; cf. 15:32). He also planned to go to Corinth with the same attitude. What was his attitude?

> "But I will come to you shortly, if the Lord will."
> —1 Corinthians 4:19

_____

_____

_____

_____

"Go to now, ye that say, To day or to morrow we will go into such a city, and continue there a year, and buy and sell, and get gain: Whereas ye know not what shall be on the morrow. For what is your life? It is even a vapour, that appeareth for a little time, and then vanisheth away. For that ye ought to say, If the Lord will, we shall live, and do this, or that."—James 4:13-15

Focus of the Lord's Prayer

The "Thy" Petitions:
Thy *name* be honored.
Thy *kingdom* come.
Thy *will* be done.
The Hinge:
On earth as it is in heaven.
The "Us" Petitions:
Give us *bread*.
Forgive us our *debts*.
Lead us not into *temptation*.
Deliver us from *evil*.

— 6 —

THE HINGE:
IN EARTH VERSUS IN HEAVEN

Wrapping Up the "Thy" Section

Because the Lord's Prayer is in perfect symmetry, it has seven petitions that are divided into two sections, and a "semi-conclusion" between. There are three petitions in the first section, and four in the second, with the fourth petition serving as a "hinge."

The first three petitions are called the "Thy" petitions because they center on God's glory.

The last four petitions are called the "Us" petitions.

At the end of the first three "Thy" petitions, you will find a semi-conclusion that wraps up the first section. The conclusion sums up what has been said to this point, but it is not the final summary nor the last conclusion. Because it comes in the middle of the Lord's Prayer, it is called a "semi-conclusion." It gives you an opportunity to wrap up your thoughts before you go on.

THE SYMMETRY OF THE LORD'S PRAYER

Introduction:	*Our Father*
The "Thy" Section	
"In heaven"	1. Thy name be hallowed—*worship*
	2. Thy kingdom come—*guidance*
	3. Thy will be done—*yieldedness*
Semi-conclusion:	*On earth as it is in heaven*
The "Us" Section	4. The "hinge": Give us bread—*provision*
"On earth"	5. Forgive us—*pardon*
	6. Keep us from temptation—*victory*
	7. Deliver us—*protection*
Benediction:	*Thine is the kingdom, power and all the glory.*

The semi-conclusion is, "on earth as it is in heaven." Jesus told us to ask for three things to be done "on earth as they are done in heaven." We ask for God to be glorified on sinful earth as He is worshiped in the perfection of heaven. We ask for God's principles to rule the stubborn earth as they do under His reign in heaven. We also ask for God's perfect will to be done on this imperfect earth as it is done in heaven.

Why did Jesus add this semi-conclusion, *On earth as it is in heaven?* Not to show us how far short we come in our prayer. You can look around and see that God is not always glorified on this earth. The semi-conclusion shows you how much you need to ask. It is there to stretch your prayers...to stretch your faith...to stretch your expectations. The semi-conclusion challenges you to pray so things on earth will be as they are in heaven.

"Don't ask for an earthly toast," Jesus is telling us, "ask for a heavenly banquet." Don't be satisfied with the bicycle; ask for a limousine. The semi-conclusion wants the best from God.

How is God's will done in heaven? Heaven is a perfect place and has no sin, no corruption, no sickness and no tears. There are no selfish agendas in heaven, only instantaneous obedience. So how is the will of God done in heaven?

Instantaneously. God's decisions are immediately carried out in heaven, so your petitions are to be done now.

Completely. God's purposes are fulfilled in heaven in every way, so that is your standard for obedience today.

Purposefully. God's duties are the only priority in heaven, so you give all intention to His will for today here on earth.

Continuously. God's will is always being done in heaven, so God's will is your schedule for today.

Gladly. God's plan is being happily done in heaven, so that is your attitude here on earth for today.

Eagerly. God's blueprint is anxiously sought by those in heaven, so that must be your passion for today.

Wholeheartedly. God's formula captivates every part of those in heaven, so you must seek it with your whole being for today and every day of your life.

The first half of the Lord's Prayer is centered on God. These are called the "Thy" petitions. When you talk to God, you must focus on Him. First, "*Thy* name be hallowed." Second, "*Thy* kingdom come." Third, "*Thy* will be done."

THE "THY" PETITIONS:
ACKNOWLEDGING GOD'S TOTAL SOVEREIGNTY

1. Because God is holy...*Thy name be hallowed*
2. Because God rules...*Thy kingdom come*
3. Because God is sovereign...*Thy will be done*

The "Thy" sections show that prayer is talking to God, not selfishly running into God's presence to beg for things you need. You tell God you want His name glorified on earth, as He is the center of worship in heaven. You tell God you want His principles done on earth, just as He reigns in heaven. You tell God you submit to His plan and purpose, as everything in heaven submits to His will.

The fourth petition is the hinge petition. A hinge is attached to two things to hold them together. The hinge petition in the Lord's Prayer, "Give us this day our daily bread," holds together the "Thy" petitions and the "Us" petitions—while serving also as the first "Us" petition.

You cannot focus on the "Thy" petitions without a strong body. So you ask for "bread" to make you physically strong. "Bread" is a symbol word that stands for all the physical things we need in this life. The hinge petition asks for a strong physical life.

The hinge is attached to the last four petitions, which consist of prayer for our spiritual walk with God. You can't ask for the last three petitions until you establish the priorities of the first three petitions. The hinge petition is a request for physical ability to do things both "in earth" and "in heaven." You can ask for "bread" only after you worship His name, live by Kingdom principles, and submit to His will in your life. Then you ask for "bread" to have the physical ability to fulfill a spiritual walk with God on this earth (i.e., to be forgiven of sin, to be victorious over sin and to be protected from the evil one).

The hinge separates the heavenly petitions from the earthly petitions, yet as only a hinge uniquely ties things together, the hinge helps you to live on earth by heavenly standards.

THE "US" PETITIONS:
ACKNOWLEDGING OUR TOTAL DEPENDENCE ON GOD

1. Because we have physical needs...*give us bread*
2. Because we sin...*forgive us our debts*
3. Because we stray...*lead us not into temptation*
4. Because we need to stand against sin...*deliver us from the evil one*

You hallow God's name (first section) when you are forgiven, victorious and protected from evil (second section).

You let God's kingdom rules come on earth (first section) when you are forgiven, victorious and protected from the evil one (second section).

You do God's will (first section) when you properly deal with past sins, you are not led into future sins and you are protected daily from the evil one (second section).

A hinge allows doors to open...and to close. The hinge of the Lord's Prayer opens up the mysteries of God so you can see how every petition interacts with one another.

The hinge allows you to swing in...and out. A child swinging on a door can pretend he or she is on an airplane or sailing a five-masted pirate's sailing ship. The swinging door allows us to go anywhere we want to go.

When you grab the semi-conclusion, you pray to God on earth as though you were "in heaven." You grab the hinge and ask God "in heaven" to answer for you even though you are living "on earth."

The hinge is real and you ask for real things. You don't live in your imagination, nor can you "make up" the conditions of prayer. The child swinging on the door never really flies and never really sails. The child only does it in his or her mind. Eventually, every child must "come down to earth" and live in the real world. So we pray *as though* we are "in heaven," but we must live "on earth."

> We must pray as though
> it all depends on God.
> We must live as though
> it all depends on us.

PRAYER CHECKLIST

This prayer checklist gives you an opportunity to review how you are applying the first three petitions of the Lord's Prayer. Take a moment to assess your spiritual growth.

In earth as it is in heaven *List how you want answers* *to your requests on earth.*	How are you doing? (check one)		
	Lousy	*Average*	*Great*
1. Has God's name been hallowed in your life?			
2. Have you asked and seen God's kingdom come into your life?			
3. Have you submitted to God's will and has it been done on earth?			

Journaling

If you are serious about touching God by daily praying the Lord's Prayer, you should have kept a record as you have prayed the first three petitions. Now is a good time to review your progress. Look over your past journal entries and answer the following questions:

1. What have you learned about worshiping God? How have you praised God? What has worship done to your personal growth and walk with God?

2. What have you learned about the principles by which God directs His kingdom work in the world today? List some of the principles of prayer you have learned. Because we should be living by God's principles, in what areas do you need to learn and grow?

3. You should do the will of God every day. What has praying daily the Lord's Prayer taught you about God's will? Write some clear aspects of God's will that you have learned. In what areas of God's will for your life do you need to learn and grow?

Three-Step Bible Study

Reviewing the "Thy" Petitions

The following Bible study is designed to help you review the "Thy" petitions so that you will gain insight and apply these truths to your life. Step 1—Read the question and try to answer it. Step 2—Read the Bible verse printed in the box, then try to determine how the Scriptures answer the question. Step 3—Write the answers in the space provided.

1. What should be our first concern when we begin praying the Lord's Prayer?

> "Our Father which art in heaven, hallowed [holy] be thy name."—Matthew 6:9
>
> "Father, glorify thy name. Then came there a voice from heaven, saying, I have both glorified it, and will glorify it again."—John 12:28

_____

_____

_____

_____

2. When we say "Our Father," we come into prayer with Jesus. How did Jesus approach prayer?

> "Father, the hour is come; glorify thy Son, that thy Son also may glorify thee:....that they might know thee the only true God, and Jesus Christ, whom thou hast sent."
> —John 17:1,3

_____

_____

_____

_____

3. When we pray "Thy kingdom come," we are asking for the Kingdom principles to rule our lives. What characterizes the Kingdom principles?

> "For the kingdom of God is not meat and drink; but righteousness, and peace, and joy in the Holy Ghost."
> —Romans 14:17

_____

_____

_____

_____

4. The prayer "Thy kingdom come" means God's rule should control our lives on earth as it does in heaven. What is our attitude?

> "Seek not ye what ye shall eat, or what ye shall drink, neither be ye of doubtful mind. For all these things do the nations of the world seek after: and your Father knoweth that ye have need of these things. But rather seek ye the kingdom of God; and all these things shall be added unto you."—Luke 12:29-31

_____

_____

_____

_____

5. The prayer "Thy will be done" is a prayer of submission. What should be our attitude?

> "If any man will come after me, let him deny himself, and take up his cross daily, and follow me."—Luke 9:23

_____

_____

_____

6. What should we yield to God?

> "Don't yield the members of your body as instruments of unrighteousness to do sin, but yield your whole self to God, as someone who is alive from the dead, and yield your bodily members as instruments of righteousness to God."—Romans 6:13 (author's translation)

_____

_____

_____

_____

7. Does God rule in heaven or on earth?

"The Lord hath prepared his throne in the heavens; and his kingdom ruleth over all."—Psalm 103:19

_____

_____

_____

8. What is happening in heaven?

"Thou, even thou, art Lord alone; thou hast made heaven, the heaven of heavens, with all their host, the earth, and all things that are therein, the seas, and all that is therein, and thou preservest them all; and the host of heaven worshippeth thee."—Nehemiah 9:6

_____

_____

_____

9. Everything on earth does not do God's will as it is done in heaven. What shall be our response?

"Now the God of peace, that brought again from the dead our Lord Jesus, that great shepherd of the sheep, through the blood of the everlasting covenant, make you perfect in every good work to do his will, working in you that which is wellpleasing in his sight, through Jesus Christ; to whom be glory for ever and ever. Amen."—Hebrews 13:20,21

_____

_____

_____

THE LORD'S PRAYER

Thy Petitions	Hinge	Us Petitions
To glorify God	For my needs	For my growth in grace
The purpose of prayer	Provision of prayer	Plan of prayer
Father/King/Master	Bread	Savior/Guide/Protector
Eternity	Now	Past/present/future
My worship of God	My needs supplied	My relationship with God
PRAISE	PROMISE	PERSONAL
Prostrate before Him	With outstretched hands	With bended neck
Looking up	Looking without	Looking within
With my hands toward God	With my hands on the plow	With my hands in His
God the Father/King	God the Farmer/Provider	God the Savior/Protector
With other worshipers in the Temple	With other workers in the world	With other walkers in this journey
In Psalms praising God	In Proverbs working in God	In Romans fellowshipping with God
Doctrine of God	Doctrine of man	Doctrine of salvation
Man directed by God	God directed to man	God and man directed to each other

The Heart of the Lord's Prayer

Hallowed be Thy name...The PRAISE of God
Thy kingdom come...The PURPOSE of God
Thy will be done...The PLAN of God
Give us bread...The PROVISION of God
Forgive us our debts...The PARDON of God
Lead us not into temptation...The POWER of God
Deliver us from the evil one...The PROTECTION of God

～ 7 ～

THE FOURTH
PETITION:
GIVE US BREAD

Asking for Things

Our evening meal was a tuna casserole—not my favorite, but it was cheap. A can of tuna cost about a quarter, and noodles were a nickel a package (1953 prices). The proverbial cupboard was bare.

My wife Ruth and I bowed our heads to thank God for our daily bread. In front of us were the casserole, a few slices of bread, iced tea and a Jell-O salad—a simple meal at the end of the day. God had always taken care of us, and we had enough "daily bread" for that day.

Nothing for tomorrow. It was about three days until the next payday.

I was a senior in college, studying for the ministry. I drove a school bus for $1 per hour. That was not the best of jobs even in 1953, but it was all I could get to fit my hours. Between studying for classes and working in a church, there was not much time to make money. I brought home about $20 a week. In those days I believed my wife should not work, so she was a full-time student along with me.

"Thank you for this food," I prayed over the tuna casserole. I was truly thankful for God's provision for that day, and knew that He would take care of tomorrow. I did not know how, though.

"You know our need," I told God. I hesitated, looking for words. "We don't have any money."

You don't need long prayers for God to answer. God can hear the shortest cry for help, and do something in response.

"Give us daily bread...."

No sooner had I said "Amen" and we saw a laundry truck drive up to our place. Ruth went to the front door. Our laundryman was a neighbor, and also our landlord. He did not own our house, he just collected rent for the owner.

"I don't have any dry cleaning today," Ruth told the laundryman, and smiling she added, "and if we gave you dirty clothes, we couldn't pay for it."

"Oh no," he told her. "I didn't come to pick up cleaning." He explained that he had been going over our rental account the previous night.

"I came to bring your money," he explained. "I didn't pay you for unplugging the pipes."

Reaching into his pocket, he took out $25 and handed it to Ruth. There had been a hard freeze when we first moved into our Minnesota home four months earlier. The temperature had plunged to 40 degrees below zero, and the bathroom pipes had frozen, so I borrowed a blowtorch from the school-bus company to thaw them. "I should have paid you three months ago," the laundryman told Ruth.

We put the $25 next to the tuna casserole and prayed again: "Thank You for our daily bread."

God provided miraculously for us, but in this case he used a job I had done earlier when we had needed water. I had worked all day to thaw the pipes. God's timing is always perfect. Three months earlier I had done what I had to do. In our hour of need, God reminded the laundryman about the $25 he owed us.

When we pray "Give us this day our daily bread," we are asking for more than "bread," although the petition includes our daily food. "Bread" is a symbol word that stands for all our physical needs. Bread gives us strength to walk...work...dig...or type at the word processor. Bread gives us stamina that drives us to close a business deal. Bread keeps our minds clear to think and to make long-range plans for our employer. Bread gives the teacher energy to handle restless children.

Bread stands for more than food. It stands for the results we get from eating food. It stands for all the physical things we need in life.

"Bread" is a symbol word that stands for money...for time...for a job...for material things. Bread stands for the roof over our heads and the clothes on our backs. It stands for a car to give us basic transportation, or subway money to get us to work. Bread stands for fuel oil in the winter...for air conditioning in the summer...for physical healing so we can work...for a raise so we can properly support our families. Bread stands for every physical need in our lives.

When you pray "Give us this day our daily bread," you recognize five factors about your needs in relationship to God.

FIVE ESSENTIAL FACTS
ABOUT OUR DAILY NEEDS

1. We have daily needs
2. God supplies our needs
3. We must ask God to supply our needs
4. Our needs are supplied one day at a time
5. We don't have to pray *for* everything, but we have to pray *about* everything

---

A salesman who attended my Bible class always wore a hat to work, although he worked in the appliance section of the department store. Everyone knew him as the tall man wearing the straw hat, white shirt and tie, and sleeves rolled up past the elbows. People thought he wore the straw hat everywhere because he was bald. Although he was bald, that was not why he wore the hat.

He had an infectious smile and liked talking to people. The best thing about him, though, was that he was a good salesman. He had a "patterned" way of closing a sale. When people said no, he would shake his head as though he did not believe what he had just heard. Then he would take off that straw hat, wipe his brow with his forearm and look inside his hat. Pausing, he would stare into his hat for a few seconds. Then he answered the objection and made the sale. No one ever asked what he was doing when he looked into his hat. It was just a habit he had acquired. Then, holding the hat for the rest of the presentation, he usually closed the sale. He did not put his hat back on till the customer left.

After I had taught the Lord's Prayer in my Bible class several years ago, the bald-headed salesman came up to me one day after class to tell me the secret of his sales ability. He made me promise not to tell anyone because most of his customers were Christians and he did not want them to attach any "magic" to his practice of removing his hat when he closed a sale. He wore his hat for one reason, he told me. A written prayer was attached to the inside of the hat band. When he looked inside his hat, he was praying what was written there: *Give us this day our daily bread.*

He explained that every sale was his "daily bread" to feed his family. He prayed that prayer while looking into the hat, then he continued praying the Lord's Prayer till the sale was finalized.

GROWING MORE BREAD, BUT EVER HUNGRIER

Realistically, most Americans who buy this book are not really hungry. They don't pray, "Give me a meal today or I'll go hungry." America is a land of abundance. We have many restaurants, fast-food outlets and grocery stores. If anything, most Americans pray, "Lord, help me lose weight."

Of course, that is not the complete picture. Many homeless Americans do not have enough to eat, and around the world millions go to bed hungry. Many who pray "Give us this day our daily bread" have an intense problem.

Most of us who walk into the supermarket have a wide variety of bread choices such as sliced bread, whole-wheat bread, rye bread, multigrain bread and rolls of various kinds. Bread is sold in various brands, sizes and prices. We can buy homemade bread, day-old bread and bread from the freezer ready to cook in our ovens. So when we pray "Give us bread," it may seem to be a rather remote and strange prayer.

Why?

Because we have taken bread for granted. Bread is so plentiful that it could be supplied to everyone who needs it.

In our technological and scientific world, we have produced more bread and more of many other kinds of food than we could ever imagine.

Take corn, for example. Our agricultural science has produced more ears per cornstalk, more cornstalks that can grow closer together and more kernels of corn per ear, producing a greater yield than any nation in the world, any time in history. Now researchers are trying to develop corn that will recycle itself each year so farmers do not have to plant it. They are producing corn that will make nitrogen to naturally fertilize itself. Maybe in the future we will harvest corn as simply as picking fruit off a tree. All this means we produce more corn than has ever been produced in the past.

America has enough farm machinery to harvest more corn than ever before. America has enough expensive combines that they could, if lined up, harvest all of Iowa in one day.

If America harvested corn as the rest of the world does, it would take 31 million people using 61 million horses to harvest Iowa in a day.

America produces enough corn to fill enough boxcars to stretch around the world several times. Our food production alone is worth $100 billion annually, an amount that staggers the imagination. So to pray "Give us this day our daily bread" does not seem like a major prayer request.

What if you had no bread? Imagine you have not had any bread for a couple of days. If you needed bread more than anything else, then you would ask for bread with all of your heart. You would pray with intensity, "Give us this day our daily bread."

America has more *physical* bread than any nation in the world. What about spiritual bread? Are we using our physical bread for the right reasons? Can we use physical bread to feed the multitudes both physically and spiritually? Perhaps one hunger feeds the other, but which one comes first?

WE HAVE DAILY NEEDS

When God created people, He did not make them like a perpetual motion machine that needs no fuel, no maintenance and no supervision. A perpetual motion machine does not need a person to run it. It needs nothing.

God did not create self-sufficient people. He created people that need air to breathe and food to give them energy. They need shelter from the elements and clothes to keep them warm. They need love to make them whole and social relationships to make them happy.

God created people to have needs. They need food, shelter, clothes and many other things. Perhaps God made people to have needs so when they stray away from Him, their needs would make them turn to Him.

People need to look outside themselves to acquire food or clothing. If they had no needs, they could just hide in a hole to hibernate the way a polar bear hides all winter. People who are hibernating in a hole, however, cannot bring glory to God. They have not found their purpose for living.

As a small boy, my mother taught me the Westminster Catechism. We attended a small Presbyterian church where the children lined up in front of the room at Sunday School to recite the children's catechism. The boys stood on one side and the girls on the other side. It was always the boys against the girls. When we missed an answer, we had to sit down. I never won—Albert Freurdt always won. Today Albert is a professor of church history at the Reformed Theological Seminary in Jackson, Mississippi.

I always wanted to answer the first question because it was easy.

The First Question in the Westminster Catechism

Q: What is the chief end of man?
A: The chief end of man is to glorify God and enjoy Him forever.

My last name is Towns, so I was always at the end of the line and had to answer the tough questions.

That first catechism question we faced in our Sunday School is the basic question of life: Why am I here? We are on this earth to bring glory to God, which we do in several ways. One of the ways is how we take care of ourselves and provide for our needs.

God made us to have needs so we would look to Him to supply them.

If we did not need bread, most people would not work. In our toil and sweat, however, we find meaning, happiness and money to buy bread.

If we did not need bread, most people would sit down and do nothing. We do not glorify God by doing nothing.

If we did not need bread, we would not create new ways of doing things; we would not invent easier ways of doing things; we would not use all the intelligence God has given us.

Because we have needs, we grow...we get better...we reach out to others...we produce...we do what God originally told Adam to do in the garden: "Be fruitful, and multiply, and replenish the earth, and subdue it: and have dominion over...every living thing" (Gen. 1:28).

Then, to make sure people understood what He meant, God explained where bread comes from: "Behold, I have given you every herb bearing seed, which is upon the face of all the earth, and every tree,...yielding seed; to you it shall be for meat" (v. 29).

GOD SUPPLIES OUR NEEDS

Most people eat bread to satisfy their personal needs...to make them grow...to make them feel better...to give them strength...or to over-come hunger. Although all this is fine, there is a bigger goal. Paul tell us, "Whether therefore ye eat, or drink, or whatsoever ye do, do all to the glory of God" (1 Cor. 10:31).

You should eat bread to glorify God because He provided every-thing. He is glorified every time you eat. That is because He created it and He gave it life to grow. He gave people the strength and intel-ligence to harvest it and He is glorified when we cook it and bow our heads before a meal to thank Him for it. Eating is for the glory of God; therefore, remember where you got your bread, who gave bread to you and what its purpose is.

When you pray "Give us this day our daily bread," you are not yanking on a string to get God's attention. Too often we treat prayer as manipulating puppet strings for our Divine Giver to give us things such as bread.

Some people wrongly pray like spoiled children, "Give me bread *now!"* They expect God, like a doting parent, to give them immediately whatever they demand. This lowers God below the human level. This approach to the Lord's Prayer is blasphemous. This treatment makes God seem like a welfare officer or the person who answers our 911 phone call.

Praying "Give us this day our daily bread" is a faith statement that is broader than asking for a sandwich. Because "bread" is a symbol word, you are asking God to bless your work so you can grow grain to make bread, or earn money to buy bread. You are asking God to give you both the *cause* (how you get physical things) and the *results* (the food you need to eat).

So when you pray "Give us this day our daily bread," you are talking with God about your needs. You are allowing God to take His rightful place in your life. Prayer is a platform to glorify God.

When you prayed the first three petitions, you set God in His rightful place in the heavens and in your heart on earth. In the first three petitions, you prayed that God's name would be hallowed, that His kingdom principles would come and that His will would be done both in heaven and on earth.

How can these three petitions be done "on earth"? First, when you pray "Give us bread," you are asking for bread that is grown on this earth. Hence, when you ask for bread, you are recognizing that God is its source, and you are worshiping His name for supplying you with bread.

Second, you are asking for God's kingdom principles to be realized on earth by the provision of food. When you pray "Thy will be done," you ask for God's plan in your life, which is working for bread, cooking bread, eating it to be strong so you can do His will and sharing it with others who are in need.

When you pray "Give us bread," you are bringing God into humanity's daily struggle for survival. When you pray "Forgive us our debts," you bring Him into your daily struggle with sin. When you pray "Lead us not into temptation," you bring Him into your struggle for victory. When you pray "Deliver us from the evil one," you bring God into your struggle for protection.

You do not approach prayer just to get something for yourself; but you ask for bread to allow God to glorify Himself through supplying your needs.

WE MUST ASK GOD TO SUPPLY OUR NEEDS

Too often we think that prayer is like a vending machine—we pop in a coin and out comes a cold drink or a packet of peanuts. Daily bread, however, does not come from a vending machine. We do not drop a prayer in some slot and expect daily bread or anything else we want from God to pop out automatically.

Some would have us think we could demand things from God. They say we should fast to get things from God, or that we can "name it to claim it" from God. God, however, does not operate by a vending machine strategy. The bottom line in all prayer is "Hallowed be Thy name." Prayer is not what we do...what we ask...what we beg. Prayer is a way to glorify and to worship God. Prayer recognizes the sovereignty of God.

> Prayer is declaring the majesty of God
> and submitting your life to His will.

Prayer is not the persuasive words of a lawyer before a jury to get a winning verdict, whether that verdict is right or necessary. We cannot manipulate God to get the right thing or what we want.

Prayer is not like a student asking a teacher for extra time to do an assignment, or putting an apple on the teacher's desk to get a better grade. God is not a teacher who withholds a good grade. God is the sovereign Ruler of the universe, and when you pray the Lord's Prayer, you bring His glory into your life. Prayer is the platform from which you worship God.

> Prayer is more than what you ask...
> More than what you do...
> More than what you say.
> Prayer is your way of living.

God has told us to pray, "Give us this day our daily bread." Jesus has said, "Ask, and it shall be given you; seek, and ye shall find; knock, and it shall be opened unto you" (Matt. 7:7). God's plan is for us to ask.

God does not give us everything we ask, though.

Some ask for too much. They ask for cake with chocolate icing, but God gives them bread—plain white bread. Why? It could be they did not work hard enough, or it could be that was not God's purpose.

Some ask to win the lottery. They want to retire and not work any longer. It is not that God does not want to give them money and ease. He knows they would stray from Him if they had it too easy. God has to keep some people on short financial leashes to keep them faithful to Him.

Has it ever occurred to you that God does not answer some people's request for money because He can't trust them?

Some people ask today for tomorrow's bread. God's answer is, "Wait until tomorrow." God may not be saying no when our prayer is not answered. He may be saying wait. We need to learn patience and character.

Some people have asked for bread, and God never answered at all. In times of famine, Christians have starved to death. Even when they prayed for "bread," God did not answer them as they requested. Does that mean God did not hear their request for "daily bread"? Did God close His eyes to the promise that we should "Ask...seek...knock"?

No, God has a time for all of us to die, a time for all to go home and meet Him. In the providence of God, some Christians may die of starvation or without clothing. (See Hebrews 11:35-39 for those who seemed forsaken in this life.)

Always preface your request for "daily bread" with the first petition of the Lord's Prayer (i.e., that His name be hallowed in the provision of your needs). When you want God to be glorified by the provision of your needs, you leave the results up to Him.

OUR NEEDS ARE SUPPLIED ONE DAY AT A TIME

The petition "Give us this day our daily bread" has a very simple yet understandable truth. We live from day to day, we eat from day to day, because we have needs from day to day. So when you pray "Give us this day," you are telling the Father you will walk with Him one day at a time.

The phrase "this day" stresses daily patience that should characterize your life. Think of those who are stressed out with anxiety because they face the problems of tomorrow, before tomorrow comes. Is it not true that most of the problems you worry about never happen? So Jesus gives you a beautiful way to live. When you pray for bread for "this day," you are telling God that you intend to live just one day at a time.

When you pray for bread for "this day," you are expressing ultimate confidence in God. You are recognizing that He is your Father, and you are His child. Think of little children playing in the yard. It is a beautiful spring day to enjoy their tricycles. They ride without thinking of who gave them the tricycles. They romp on the grass without thinking who will mow it. They eat a sandwich without thinking of who will plant crops in the spring to grow in the summer for a full harvest. Putting bread on the table is the father's job. Mother's job is providing Kool-Aid or treats. Children have few worries because they trust their parents. When you pray for bread for "this day," you are exercising ultimate confidence in your heavenly Father to provide for your needs.

Quit worrying about what has not happened yet. Why? Because worrying about tomorrow is telling the heavenly Father you are not sure He can provide for tomorrow's "bread." "Worry" is another word for doubt. You doubt God's care when you worry about provisions.

There is a difference between worrying about tomorrow and planning for tomorrow. The Bible calls the ant "exceeding wise" because "the ants are a people not strong, yet they prepare their meat in the summer" (Prov. 30:24,25). Ants do not worry; they prepare.

WE DON'T HAVE TO PRAY *FOR* EVERYTHING, BUT WE HAVE TO PRAY *ABOUT* EVERYTHING

The Lord's Prayer does not say, "Give us this day's bread, clothes, a roof over our heads and shoes for the kids." It only commands us to pray "Give us bread" because bread is the symbol word standing for all our needs. You are to pray about your needs, but you do not have to blurt out a grocery list of them to your heavenly Father. Jesus gives us the reason when introducing the Lord's Prayer. "Your Father knoweth what things ye have need of, before ye ask him" (Matt. 6:8).

Obviously, we may have many needs on our hearts. When we come to the Father we should tell Him our concerns. The passage does not say we should not ask the Father to meet these needs. It implies the opposite by saying that God knows of these needs "before ye ask him."

When we have good health, we do not ask for good health. God knows we need good health. We thank Him for good health...for our jobs...for the enjoyable things in life.

How much bread makes up daily bread? Does God supply all we *need* or all we *want*? We can pray for necessities, but nowhere are we told to pray for luxuries. We are commanded to pray for "daily bread," but should we pray for strawberry shortcake?

The book of Proverbs gives us the answer in a principle for living. "Give me neither poverty nor riches; feed me with food convenient [appropriate] for me" (Prov. 30:8).

How much should we pray for? Daily bread is enough to get us through one day. The writer of Proverbs speaks of "convenient" food, which is enough for today. Like a convenience store, you do not go there to buy your whole week's groceries. You just go for what you need for one meal or for today. A convenience store provides for daily needs.

Why should we pray for daily bread? The writer of Proverbs continues, "Lest I be full, and deny thee, and say, Who is the Lord? or lest I be poor, and steal, and take the name of my God in vain" (v. 9). So we should not focus on tomorrow's bread, lest we forget God. When we have too much bread, we forget the source of bread, who is God.

Americans have become very rich, and it seems that the richer they become the less they attend church, pray or are fearful of breaking His laws concerning fornication, lying, stealing or any other of the Ten Commandments. Maybe if Americans were poor and hungry again, as in the Great Depression, they would cry out to God, "Give us this day our daily bread."

Yet the writer of Proverbs said he needed "food convenient for me." For without daily bread, he might become poor, and steal, and take the name of God in vain. When we do not have enough bread, our hunger can drive us to deny the God who gives us our necessities.

Although Americans are not starving physically, we are starving in other ways. We are starved in our souls, for we steal, lie and jealously hurt one another. We are starved in our character when we compromise our standards and deny God's rightful place in our society. We are starving in our families when we deny love, respect and fellowship to one another.

As a teenager, I learned a song at camp that teaches this truth: *One day at a time, sweet Jesus.*

As a youth, however, I did not understand the full meaning of what I was singing. It was just an enjoyable tune, but the song had a prayer that arises from the Lord's Prayer: *Teach me to live one day at a time.*

PRAYER CHECKLIST

Give us this day our daily bread *List the things you must pray for.*	How are you doing? (check one)		
	Lousy	*Average*	*Great*
1.			
2.			
3.			
4.			
5.			
6.			
7.			

JOURNALING

It is a good discipline to keep a record of the prayer requests you make. Which ones has God answered, and why did He answer them? What requests has He apparently not answered? Write a note to yourself explaining why you think He has not answered certain prayers. Compare the answers with the nonanswers. What can you learn?

1. Write out the things for which you pray. As you receive answers, check them off.
2. Make a list of your greatest answers to prayer last week, last month, last year. Why did God answer some prayers on your checklist, and not others?
3. Make a list of your nonanswers to prayer last week, last month, last year. Write what you learned about prayer from nonanswers.
4. Describe in your own words how you feel when God answers your prayers...and when He does not seem to answer.
5. What have you learned about the person and glory of God by praying for things?

THREE-STEP BIBLE STUDY

PRAYING FOR THINGS

The following Bible study will guide you to pray for things. Step 1—Read the question and try to answer it. Step 2—Read the Bible verse that is printed with the question, and try to determine how the Word of God answers the question. Step 3—Write the answers in the space provided.

1. Why are some of your prayer requests not answered?

"You do not have because you do not ask. You ask and do not receive, because you ask amiss [for the wrong reason], that you may spend it on your pleasures."—James 4:2,3 (NKJV)

_____

_____

_____

2. What is a primary condition of receiving answers to your prayers?

> "Now we know that God heareth not sinners: but if any man be a worshipper of God, and doeth his will, him he heareth."—John 9:31

_____

_____

_____

_____

3. Why are we to make specific requests of God? (What is the meaning of "Ask...seek...and knock"?)

> "Ask, and it shall be given you; seek, and ye shall find; knock, and it shall be opened unto you: for every one that asketh receiveth; and he that seeketh findeth; and to him that knocketh it shall be opened."—Matthew 7:7,8

_____

_____

_____

4. By what authority do you pray for things?

> "And whatsoever ye shall ask in my [Jesus'] name, that will I do, that the Father may be glorified in the Son. If ye shall ask anything in my name, I will do it."—John 14:13,14

_____

_____

_____

_____

5. What should be your attitude when you pray for things?

> "If ye abide in me, and my words abide in you, ye shall ask what ye will, and it shall be done unto you."—John 15:7

_____
_____
_____
_____

6. What is the relationship between the fruit of Christian character and receiving answers to prayer?

> "Ye have not chosen me, but I have chosen you, and ordained you, that ye should go and bring forth fruit, and that your fruit should remain: that whatsoever ye shall ask of the Father in my name, he may give it you."
> —John 15:16

_____
_____
_____

7. What is the role of faith or confidence in praying for things?

> "And this is the confidence that we have in him, that, if we ask any thing according to his will, he heareth us: and if we know that he hear us, whatsoever we ask, we know that we have the petitions that we desired of him."
> —1 John 5:14,15

_____
_____
_____

8. How long should you pray for your request?

> "And he [Jesus] spake a parable unto them to this end, that men ought always to pray, and not to faint."—Luke 18:1

_____
_____
_____
_____

9. What should you expect in prayer when you meet all
    of God's conditions?

"But without faith it is impossible to please him: for
he that cometh to God must believe that he is, and that
he is a rewarder of them that diligently seek him."
—Hebrews 11:6

_____
_____
_____
_____

Those Who Can't Pray
the Lord's Prayer

⸺ ᘒᘒ ⸺

If you don't know Christ...you can't pray, "Our Father."

If you glorify yourself...you can't pray, "Hallowed be Thy name."

If you reject His rules...you can't pray, "Thy kingdom come."

If you won't submit...you can't pray, "Thy will be done."

If your life is only for here and now...you can't pray, "On earth as it is in heaven"

If you are self-sufficient...you can't pray, "Give us our daily bread."

If you won't forgive...you can't pray, "Forgive us our debts."

If you seek sin...you can't pray, "Lead us not into temptation."

If you are a friend of evil...you can't pray, "Deliver us from evil."

If you build your own kingdom...you can't pray, "Thine is the kingdom."

If you want power...you can't pray, "Thine is the power."

If you always take credit,...you can't pray, "Thine is the glory."

~ 8 ~

THE FIFTH
PETITION:
FORGIVE US OUR DEBTS

Getting Forgiveness and Feeling Clean

John had to try out his new slingshot. He perched tin cans on the farm fence, but missed every shot. Slingshots are not very accurate even when you make them yourself. John shot at a bird in the tree, and missed. After all, he is only in the fourth grade. He shot at a rabbit and missed. He shot at the dog and missed. John was getting more frustrated by the minute.

Grandmother called him for dinner. On the way to the house, he shot at grandmother's favorite duck—and this time he hit his target. The missile hit the duck in the head, instantly killing it. No one was in the yard. John looked both ways to be sure that no one saw him. Quickly, he grabbed a shovel and ran behind the barn to bury the duck.

After dinner, Grandmother asked Sally to wash the dishes. Sally said her brother, John, wanted to wash dishes. Then she whispered to him, "Remember the duck."

Apparently, Sally had seen what happened, and blackmailed her brother. John washed the dishes.

Next morning when Grandmother asked Sally to sweep the porch, she said John wanted to sweep. Then she whispered to John again, "Remember the duck."

All that week Sally blackmailed her brother into doing her work around the house. Every time she wanted John to do a chore, she whispered, "Remember the duck."

When John could not stand any more guilt, he finally confessed to his grandmother that he had killed her favorite duck. She replied, "I was washing dishes at the window and saw you hit the duck. I know you didn't mean to do it. I could see fear in your face." She explained to John, "I forgave you the moment you did it, but I wondered how long you would live with your guilt before you told me."

Many Christians are like John. We have done something terrible, and someone like the "Sallys" of this world holds us in bondage. For others, the "Sallys" are internal. We are in slavery to our own guilt.

Many new believers rush into God's presence with their shopping list and begin to ask, "Give me this..." or "Give me that...." Although you can ask God for things, that is not the way to begin the Lord's Prayer.

Other believers want to begin their prayer with, "I'm sorry..." or "Forgive me...." They feel so guilty about a sin that they want to begin with confession. As much as sin blocks your fellowship with God, however, that is not the way to begin the Lord's Prayer.

As we have seen, first you worship God: "Hallowed be Thy name." Second, you seek to live by His kingdom principles: "Thy kingdom come in my life on earth." Third, you ask for guidance: "Thy will be done." Because you must have physical life to have spiritual life, the fourth petition is: "Give us bread for today."

When you have prayed in these four ways you are then ready to confront the sin in your life. The fifth prayer is: "Forgive us our debts," which introduces you to the "Us" petitions. You pray "Forgive us," then "Lead us not into temptation" and finally, "Deliver us from the evil one."

This chapter is concerned with the sins that block your fellowship with God.

When you pray "Forgive us our debts," you are recognizing five factors of the Christian life.

FIVE ESSENTIAL FACTS ABOUT OUR SIN

1. God's children sin
2. God's children are concerned after they sin
3. God's children must do something about their sin
4. God will forgive
5. Forgiving others is essential, too

When you pray "Forgive us our debts," you are not begging for salvation as does the non-Christian who feels the guilt of hell.

When you pray "Forgive us our debts," you are not saying your sin has cast away all hope and that you are afraid of dying outside of Christ.

When you pray "Forgive us our debts," you are praying as a child of the Father who has not lived up to your Father's expectation. You are saying "I'm sorry" to your heavenly Father so you can have fellowship with Him again.

"Forgive us our debts" is not *initial forgiveness*, which is the sinner coming to God for salvation. Many mistakenly think this prayer is asking God to make them Christians. Not so! When you pray "Forgive us our debts," you already are a Christian who calls God "our Father." You already are a child of the King...you are in the Kingdom.

When you pray "Forgive us our debts," you are asking for "parental forgiveness." Because you are a child of the Father, you are related to Him by nature. You received a new nature at salvation (see 2 Cor. 5:17). You can call God your Father. You are a member of the family of God.

Suppose a child sneaks behind his father's back and does what his father told all the children not to do. Is the father no longer the child's father? The answer is obviously no! A child is a member of his father's family by birth. Disobeying his father does not break the father/child *relationship*, but the fellowship between father and child. The relationship is intact, but the father is disappointed.

We became children of our heavenly Father by the new birth. Just as fathers on earth are "crushed" when their children go wrong, so God's heart is broken when His children disobey Him. No wonder we feel guilt. We have let our Father down. When we pray "Forgive us our debts," however, we are asking the Father God to restore our *fellowship* with Him, not to restore the Father/child *relationship*.

GOD'S CHILDREN SIN

The Lord's Prayer teaches us that God's children do not always do God's will. The Father does tell His children, "Be ye...perfect" (Matt. 5:48). It is something like a mother bragging to her friends, "My children are perfect angels"; the potential is there, but she knows better. She was late to the luncheon because her children spilled a cola when sneaking it out of the refrigerator...she had told them "not before lunch."

The earthly father tells his son, "Don't do anything wrong," just as the Scripture tells us, "My little children, these things write I unto you, that ye sin not" (1 John 2:1). When you pray "Forgive us our debts," you are admitting that you sin. No one is perfect: "All have sinned" (Rom. 3:23). We sin, and break fellowship with the Father, in several ways.

First, we break fellowship with God by disobeying Him.

A father asks his son to wash the family car and sweep out the floorboards. The son forgets, though, and neglects to do it. When the son asks the father to borrow the car for a date, a wise father says, "No...." The father has a lesson to teach his son. "You didn't wash the car like I asked, so you can't borrow the car for a date."

Second, we break fellowship with God when we do the opposite of God's command.

The father sends his son on an errand in the family car. He tells the son, "Be careful, and get the car washed, and pick up the groceries." The son scrapes a fender, drives through mud and leaves burger wrappers on the floor. He forgets to pick up the groceries. He does the opposite of what his father asked. When the son asks to borrow the car for a date, he hears the same thing.

"No...," the father replies. "You were not careful and you didn't wash it."

Third, we break fellowship with God by ignoring Him. A son never comes to family meals, never goes anywhere with Dad and generally ignores his father. When the time comes for the son's big date, he asks for the family car.

"No...," the father replies. "You don't spend time with the family when it means something to us. Why should I help you have fun?"

All three sons have disappointed their fathers. They are still their fathers' sons, and their actions have not broken the relationship. However, they have broken their fellowship with their fathers.

A loving father would probably lend them the car if they said, "I'm sorry," and if they showed a change of attitude, maybe by washing and waxing the car.

When you pray "Forgive us our debts," you are asking forgiveness for the little petty things you sneak around to do, as well as the massive rebellion that breaks God's heart. You do not want to hurt your heavenly Father; it is just that you want to do what you think is fun...or exciting...or new...or different...or to relieve boredom. You just want to do what you want to do...when you want to do it...for your own selfish reasons.

There is a reason why you pray "Forgive us our *debts*." The word "debt" represents how much we owe to someone. A debt is an obligation. So you are really praying, "Forgive us our obligations."

If you borrow money, you have an obligation to repay it. If you back into someone's car, you have an obligation to repair the fender. If you spill a milkshake on someone's new coat, you have an obligation to have it cleaned. If you sin against God, you have an obligation to Him.

Why does the Lord's Prayer use this word for obligations, or debts, instead of "sins"?

The basic meaning of the New Testament word for sin is "to miss the mark." Jesus did not tell us to pray "Forgive us our sin" (i.e., where we missed the mark, because our failures were forgiven when we became Christians).

Jesus did not tell us to pray "Forgive us our transgressions" (i.e., where we ruthlessly rebelled against God). Our rebellion was forgiven when we repented to become Christians.

Jesus did not tell us to pray "Forgive us our lawlessness" (i.e., our contempt for God's law). That is because when we recognized God's perfect law, we realized how we disobeyed Him.

Jesus did not tell us to pray "Forgive us our moments of passion" (i.e., the times we slip or fall). That is because, "If we walk in the light,...the blood of Jesus Christ [God's] Son cleanseth us from all sin" (1 John 1:7). That cleansing is automatic.

Jesus did not tell us to pray "Forgive us our wickedness" (i.e., our filthiness). That sin is forgiven when we become Christians.

The Lord's Prayer says, "Forgive us our *debts*" (i.e., our obligations), because we need to be forgiven not only for our sins, but also their consequences—the obligations we have incurred.

When you get so mad you slap your child, that is a sin against God and against the child. God forgives your anger, but what about your child? You have an obligation to your child to seek forgiveness. So you pray, "Forgive us our debts—our obligations—as we forgive our debtors."

Jesus taught us to pray "Forgive us our debts" because of the sins that involve other people. A "debt" is a sin containing fine print. When you sign a contract, read the fine print. It may obligate you for more money than you agreed to in the big print.

When you tell a lie, it hurts your self-esteem, it hurts another and it offends God. When you tell a lie, the fine print means you are obligated to go apologize to someone.

If you cheat on your spouse, you hurt yourself, you break one of the commandments and you have broken your obligation to your spouse. So you pray, "Forgive me my debt-obligation to my wife."

The Lord's Prayer is perfect. Jesus chose the perfect word for forgiveness. It is our debt—obligations—that must be forgiven.

SIX NEW TESTAMENT WORDS FOR SIN				
Word	Greek	Meaning	Explanation	Scripture
1. Sin	*harmartia*	to miss the mark	inability to do good	Romans 3:23
2. Transgress	*parabaino*	to step across the line	no restraint	2 John 9
3. Lawlessness	*anomia*	open, flagrant rejection	contempt of law	1 John 3:4
4. Trespass	*paraptoma*	a falling or slipping	passion of moment	Matthew 6:14
5. Debt	*opheilema*	what is owed; obligation	consequences of sin	Matthew 6:12
6. Wickedness	*poneria*	wicked desire	filthiness	Matthew 22:18

GOD'S CHILDREN ARE
CONCERNED AFTER THEY SIN

Not all people feel guilty when they disobey the Father. Some take God's name in vain, then laugh. Some commit adultery because it feels good, then do it again. Some get so drunk to hide their problems that they become addicted. There is always the prodigal son who leaves home for more exciting experiences. He turns his back on his father and, seemingly, never looks back.

If you are a child of the Father, however, you can't sin...at least you can't sin continually...and not suffer some inner guilt.

A young Chinese girl was employed by missionaries to clean house while the missionaries were busy with their ministry in inland China. The young girl, however, would steal little things. It was a cultural thing. Her fetish religion taught her that she had the "spirit" of the missionaries when she had their possessions. So she stole personal things such as buttons, handkerchiefs and broaches. The missionaries knew what she did, and every day went through the young girl's things before she left. She had no guilt about stealing. If anything, it was a prized cultural thing to do.

In time, the young girl was converted and began to grow in Christ. She was taught not to steal, along with other Christian principles. After a period of time, the young house girl saw a golden locket, knew it meant much to the missionary, and was tempted. She wanted the locket and tried it on; then she put it back on the dresser. She returned several times to try it on; and finally she stole it.

In the middle of the night when the missionaries were sound asleep, the young girl banged on the door. When they opened the door she burst in, threw the locket on the floor, sobbing, and said, "I'm not a Christian...!" Between sobs the girl kept saying, "I'm sorry!" The wife sent her husband back to bed. Then in a spirit of love she explained to the young Chinese girl what it meant to have God's nature. She explained that before the young girl was a Christian, she stole things, but then stealing did not bother her. Now that she had a new nature in Christ, she felt guilt.

If you are guilty because you have disobeyed the heavenly Father, you should pray, "Forgive us our debts." Granting forgiveness when you ask is the Father's way of handling your guilt.

You may have sinned at some point, but you have forgotten about it. You may not have always been perfect...you may not have done all the Father's will...or you may have ignorantly disobeyed the Father. Pray daily "Forgive us our debts" to take care of any sin that may have innocently crept into your life. You need to take care of any sin you may have ignorantly committed.

No one should stubbornly refuse to pray "Forgive us our debts" because that proud attitude may keep the person from fellowship with the Father. When you pray "Forgive us our debts," God may use this prayer to reveal a hidden sin or a sin you were not aware of. That sin may have blocked your ability to talk to Him.

Sin denies God's purity; it dirties us.
Sin ignores God's honor; it embarrasses us.
Sin disobeys God's command; it condemns us.
Sin violates God's law; it makes criminals of us.
Sin corrupts God's health; it sickens us.
Sin steals God's blessing; it robs us.
Sin disrupts God's peace; it makes us guilty.
For our sin we pray, Forgive us.

Guilt robs you of two things: heaven and health. First, if God is not your Father, your guilt will rob you of the Father's heavenly home. If you are not a child of the Father, you need to believe in Jesus Christ. He said, "I am the way, the truth, and the life: no man cometh unto the Father, but by me" (John 14:6).

You may be the Father's child, yet disobeyed the Father, and now you feel guilty. Lying brings an internal nausea, for no one can lie to oneself. You can lie to your friends, your mother, your wife, but you can't lie to yourself. If you are mentally healthy, you know what is true. We feel guilty when we are caught stealing. We feel guilty when we do not live up to our standards. We are embarrassed when we are caught lying because the truth is out. Guilt produces self-doubt, anxiety, stress and, in accelerated cases, leads to neuroses and phobias. Guilt is soul sickness.

When you pray daily "Forgive us our debts," you are taking a step toward mental health. When you ask for forgiveness, you are telling the truth to yourself and to God. You are restoring your self-respect and your relationship with God. When you feel good about yourself, it shows in your relationships, in your job, in your walk with God; but most of all it shows in your earthly family.

You pray "Forgive us our debts," however, not just to feel better or to grow in personal strength. You pray it to restore your fellowship with the heavenly Father...if it is broken...and to keep it healthy if you have not broken it. You pray this prayer for a healthy relationship with the Father.

The prodigal son demanded his family inheritance. He was callous to the feelings of his father and his brother. He wanted a different style of life. He turned his back on them and walked away without looking back. Everything went wrong, though. He lost his money, his worldly friends and his self-respect. He ended up feeding hogs. There, in the hogpen, the prodigal son's thinking turned back to his father. He thought about his father before he physically returned home.

If you are far away from God, turn your thoughts to God. Pray, "Forgive me my debts," and begin the journey home.

WHY PRAY "FORGIVE US"?

Sin is the wound of the heart
    that makes you weep.
Sin is the virus of mental health
    that makes your soul sick.
Sin is the original pollution of the human body
    that causes your sickness and death.
Sin is the misunderstanding between couples
    that breaks up marriages.
Sin is the selfishness of desire
    that destroys your character.
Sin is the suspicion of motives
    that shatters friendship.

GOD'S CHILDREN MUST DO SOMETHING ABOUT THEIR SIN

When you pray daily "Forgive us our sins," you are beginning to do something about your guilt and the broken fellowship with your Father.

The young boy who killed his grandmother's duck went to her and confessed it. The boy who refused to wash his father's car had to say, "I'm sorry." The young cleaning girl returned the locket sobbing, "I'm sorry." The prodigal son came to his senses in the hogpen when he said, "My father's servants are treated better than this."

Simply repeating or reading the words "Forgive us our debts" is not enough. Paul explains, "Godly sorrow worketh repentance" (2 Cor. 7:10). Godly sorrow is meaning it with your heart, meaning it so deeply you never want to do it again.

When a thief is caught and sentenced to jail, he is sorry. He may even promise never to steal again. Habitual thieves are sorry about the wrong thing, though. They are sorry they were caught. They are not sorry they have broken the law—either God's law or the people's law. That is why most thieves will steal again if given the opportunity. Being sorry only if we are caught is what Paul calls "the sorrow of the world [that] worketh death" (v. 10).

"Godly sorrow" is the sorrow experienced by a thief who plans never to steal again.

When you pray daily "Forgive us our debts," it must be followed with an outward change or determination to change. What you mean in your heart will change your actions. When a child tells his earthly father he is sorry for dashing out into the street, the father wants the son never to do it again. This is not because the father is legalistic or wants to curb the boy's fun. The father does not want his son hurt in traffic.

So also does the heavenly Father want us to confess inwardly and repent outwardly. He does not want us to get hurt.

> Confess inwardly.
> Repent outwardly.

GOD WILL FORGIVE

If you confess your sins, God will forgive them, just because He said so. "If we confess our sins, he is faithful and just to forgive us our sins, and to cleanse us from all unrighteousness" (1 John 1:9).

When you pray "Forgive us our debts," you are exercising belief or trust in God. You confess your sins because you believe God will forgive you as He promised. You confess your sins because you know God will forgive you.

> Who is a God like unto thee, that pardoneth iniquity, and passeth by the transgression of the remnant...? he delighteth in mercy. He will turn again, he will have compassion upon us;...thou wilt cast all their sins into the depths of the sea (Mic. 7:18,19).

You should pray "Forgive us our debts" because it feels good to be clean and refreshed. It feels like a warm shower that washes away sweat and dirt after cutting the grass. It feels like a relaxing quick snooze on the couch when you first get home from a stressful day. It feels like the loving embrace of parent and child. You can get forgiveness for what you have done, and it will feel good. You do not confess to feel good; you confess to be forgiven, but forgiveness feels good.

> We need forgiveness to be happy.
> We need forgiveness to be mentally healthy.

The Bible says that forgiveness is God taking away our sin (see John 1:29). Forgiveness is God covering our sin (see Ps. 85:2). Forgiveness is God blotting out our sin (see Isa. 43:25). Forgiveness is God forgetting our sin (see Mic. 7:19).

> The Father already has forgiven us.
> The Father waits to cleanse us.

Why should we pray "Forgive us our debts" when all our sins were forgiven at the Cross? When we become a child of the Father, the Bible says, "We have redemption through his blood, the forgiveness of sins" (Eph. 1:7). If our sins were forgiven at salvation, why pray daily, "Forgive us"?

The initial forgiveness of sins established our *relationship* to God. It made us children of the Father. When, as sinful children, we pray "Forgive us," it reestablishes our *fellowship* with the Father. Because children do not always obey, you need to pray daily, "Forgive us our debts."

There are three aspects to forgiveness, not just one or two. First there is *past* forgiveness, which happened when we became children of the Father. When God forgave our past sins, our relationship with God was established.

Second, there is *present* forgiveness, which happens every time you pray "Forgive us our debts," and God reestablishes our fellowship with the Father.

The third aspect is *future* forgiveness. This will happen when we are taken to be with the Father, whether by death or when the Lord comes. This will be our glorification when we are removed from all traces of evil and decay on this earth.

FORGIVING OTHERS IS ESSENTIAL, TOO

When you pray "Forgive us our debts as we forgive our debtors," immediately you bring other people into the relationship with you and the Father. You are asking God to forgive your sins as you forgive the sins of others.

Some have resisted that provision, claiming that "Forgive me as I forgive" sounds like legalism out of the Old Testament. They say it sounds like "an eye for an eye" and places a condition on God's forgiveness. It sounds as though God will forgive you only as you forgive those who sin against you. Three word pictures will help us see what the Father meant.

> Forgiveness is a ticket.
> Forgiveness is a circle.
> Forgiveness is our character.

When you fly on an airplane, you need a ticket; and like most tickets, it has two sections. The first section of the ticket says, "Good for travel—not good if detached." You give that section of the ticket to the clerk to get on the plane. The second section of the ticket is your boarding pass. It has your seat number, and it proves you have paid the fare. A boarding pass is no good without a ticket.

In a similar way, when you get saved, your sins are forgiven. This is your ticket to heaven. Remember, though, that it is not good if detached from the boarding pass. You have to do good works, which means you must forgive others as the Father has forgiven you. The second part of your ticket to heaven guarantees the price has been paid. It says, "Not good for travel." Good works won't get you to heaven. It also says, "Not good if detached." When you forgive others, it demonstrates that God has forgiven you. You demonstrate the value of the first half of the ticket by praying, "Forgive us our debts, as we forgive others."

The plane ticket illustration tells you to pray two things. First, pray each day, "Forgive us our debts," and God will forgive you. Second, the ticket tells you to pray each day, "Forgive your debtors."

> We must ask forgiveness.
> We must forgive debtors.

Forgiveness is a circle—what you give is what you get. Everything always goes in a circle and comes back to us. Jesus reminded us "to love our neighbor as we love ourselves." God does not want us to love ourselves only. Nor are we to love our neighbor only. It is impossible to do one without the other. To be loved, we must love others. The same thing is true of forgiveness. To be forgiven, you must forgive.

When we pray "Forgive us our debts," we must be ready to forgive anyone who has done the same thing to us. When we "Forgive our debtors," we must do it because God has already done His part. Notice that forgiveness begins with God. He forgives first, then we follow His example to demonstrate that we really have been forgiven. What goes around, comes around.

WHY MUST YOU FORGIVE?

Forgiveness is also a clue to our character.

A mother who had two sons died, but left the younger son as the executor of the estate. In settling the estate, he spent more than half the inheritance on trips to examine the assets, running up bills for expensive hotels and meals on extended stays. The older brother accused the younger of taking all-expense-paid vacations on his inheritance. When money is on the table, even brothers get selfish and envious.

"I'll never forgive him," the older brother said.

The brothers did not talk to one another for 15 years.

If the older brother does not "forgive his debtors," he is in bondage to his younger brother and the way the inheritance was spent. The older brother is in debt to the younger, although the younger took the money.

If the older brother does not "forgive his debtors," he refuses to let the younger off the hook, but it means the older brother is also on the hook. He is in debt to the younger brother.

If the older brother does not "forgive his debtors," he is tied to his younger brother's sin and its consequences. The older brother does not forgive his younger brother to help the younger brother feel good. He forgives the younger brother for his own healing. He does not want to be in debt to anyone for anything, at any time.

If the older brother does not "forgive his debtors," the issue is still between the brothers. However, when the older brother forgives for the Father's sake, the issue is between the younger brother and God. When you forgive others their debts, you are no longer their debtor; neither are you God's debtor. You are free.

WHY FORGIVE?

You are commanded to forgive	*Romans 12:19*
The example of Jesus	*Luke 23:34*
To prosper spiritually	*Matthew 18:35*
To be a testimony	*Colossians 3:13*
To receive forgiveness	*Matthew 6:15*

Forgiveness is not natural to a growing baby. I gave my granddaughter Kim a gourmet cookie, just because that is what grandfathers do. My daughter Polly immediately instructed Kim, "Say thank-you."

Kim stuck out her bottom lip and shook her head, "No!" Something in human nature does not want to express gratitude. My daughter Polly repeated her exhortation two or three times, but Kim became more adamant. She would not say, "Thank-you." Kim started to put the cookie in her mouth.

Polly grabbed Kim's hand that held the cookie, which Kim squeezed tighter, but my daughter would not let her hand go until Kim showed gratitude. Finally Kim said, "Thank-you." Then when Kim opened her hand, the cookie was smashed to goo. It was no longer beautiful. Sometimes we are like Kim. We refuse to be grateful for the things God has given us. When God has forgiven us, we must be grateful; and one way we show that gratitude is by forgiving others.

> Gratitude is the least remembered
> of all virtues, and the acid test of character.

PRAYER CHECKLIST

Forgive us our debts as we forgive our debtors *List the struggles of your life, and the people you must forgive.*	How are you doing? (check one)		
	Lousy	Average	Great
1.			
2.			
3.			
4.			
5.			
6.			
7.			

JOURNALING

It is always difficult to keep a record of one's sin. So do not write and describe your faults, habits or gross wickedness. Just describe in general terms how you are doing in your struggle with sin. Describe your victories, and try to go from "victory to victory." Mention also your failures, but do not stop there. Write what you do about your failures and how you plan to be victorious next time.

1. List your struggles with sin and failure. How did you feel? Why were you defeated? What do you plan to do to be victorious?
2. List your victories over sin and habits. How did you achieve victory? What principles did you learn? What were the results?
3. List the people you need to forgive. Why do you need to forgive them? Pray for the spiritual prosperity of each person on this list. When you pray for them, you can't feel a grudge against them. Praying for them makes forgiveness permanent.

THREE-STEP BIBLE STUDY

GETTING FORGIVENESS

This Bible study is designed to show you the biblical basis for getting forgiveness. Step 1—Read the question and think through the answer. Step 2—Read the Bible verse that is printed with the question, and try to determine how the Word of God answers the question. Step 3—Write the answers in the space provided.

1. All Christians sin, even Paul in his old age. What can we learn about sin from Paul's testimony?

> "This is a faithful saying, and worthy of all acceptation, that Christ Jesus came into the world to save sinners; of whom I am chief."—1 Timothy 1:15

2. Can we say we have not sinned? What about those who make that boast?

> "If we say that we have no sin [nature], we deceive ourselves, and the truth is not in us."—1 John 1:8.
> "If we say that we have not sinned [actions], we make him a liar, and his word is not in us."—1 John 1:10

3. Even though we are sinners, what does God expect of His children?

> "My little children, these things write I unto you that ye sin not."—1 John 2:1).
> "He that saith he abideth in him (Jesus) ought himself also to walk, even as he walked."—1 John 2:6

4. How can a disobedient child of God get forgiveness? What does forgiveness include?

> "If we confess our sins, he is faithful and just to forgive us our sins, and to cleanse us from all unrighteousness."
> —1 John 1:9

_____
_____
_____
_____
_____

5. Children of God do not always live up to God's standards. Sometimes they are ignorant of God's standards. How does God take care of these kinds of sins?

> "If we walk in the light, as he [Jesus] is in the light, we have fellowship one with another, and the blood of Jesus Christ his Son cleanseth us from all sin."—1 John 1:7

_____
_____
_____
_____

6. What should our attitude be toward those we sin against?

> "Therefore if thou bring thy gift to the altar, and there rememberest that thy brother hath ought against thee; leave there thy gift before the altar, and go thy way; first be reconciled to thy brother, and then come offer thy gift."—Matthew 5:23,24

_____
_____
_____
_____

7. How important is forgiving others?

> "For if ye forgive men their trespasses, your heavenly Father will also forgive you: but if ye forgive not men their trespasses, neither will your Father forgive your trespasses."—Matthew 6:14,15

_____

_____

_____

_____

8. What is the basis for all forgiveness?

"Forbearing one another, and forgiving one another, if any man have a quarrel against any: even as Christ forgave you, so also do ye."—Colossians 3:13

_____

_____

_____

_____

Martin Luther's Evening Prayer

We give thanks unto thee, heavenly Father, through Jesus Christ, thy dear Son, that thou hast this day so graciously protected us; and we beseech thee to forgive us all our sins, and the wrong which we have done, and by thy great mercy defend us from all the perils and dangers of this night. Into thy hands we commend our bodies and souls, and all that is ours. Let thy holy angel have charge concerning us, that the wicked one have no power over us. Amen.

9

THE SIXTH PETITION:
LEAD US NOT INTO TEMPTATION

Finding Victory over Barriers

I thought I saw a squirrel in the top of a live oak tree. I quietly ran to the other side, whispering to Art Winn, my high school buddy,

"Watch for him from this side."

We were squirrel hunting on our Thanksgiving break from classes. We crouched for a long time, waiting for the squirrel to come out of hiding, but the squirrel outwaited us.

We continued walking in the deep drainage ditch. We kept looking up into the tree tops for squirrels. County workers had shoveled out the ditch bottom, so it was an easy walk. The autumn day was cool. There were no bushes in the ditch, so we did not have to worry about snakes.

We came to a fork where the ditch split into two directions that ran on both sides of an "island" field—a tract of cotton ground that was surrounded by woods and ditches.

"I'll meet ya on the other side," Art told me. He took the right ditch, still looking up into the treetops for squirrels. It was a 15-minute walk before we would meet on the other side of the island field.

The sky was overcast and the cloud cover kept the squirrels out of sight. There was no sunshine to coax them out where we could find them. Then I began to hear a light rain fall on the dry leaves in the woods.

"No sun, no squirrels, and now rain," I complained.

The leaves had already fallen, so there were no leaves on the trees for protection. I figured the rain would stop shortly, so I looked for a tree that might have a large limb for protection from the chilly rain. There were none.

Then I noticed some shelter. I saw a big hole underneath the tree roots of a gigantic oak tree in the side of the ditch. It was big enough to protect me from the rain. This kind of oak has a large, flat pattern of roots. The sand underneath the roots had washed out into the ditch, leaving the hole. There are no natural caves in central South Carolina, but here was a "hole" to keep me dry.

"Arthur!" I yelled as loudly as I could for him to come keep dry. All I heard was rain on the dry leaves.

The hole was only big enough for me to lie on my side; it was not tall enough to sit or squat. My clothes were damp, and I shivered. In the corner of the hole were some dry leaves and branches the wind had blown there. I pulled them together and lit a small fire in the opposite end of the hole. I scooted around to get my shoulders and the back of my wet shirt toward the fire.

Then I saw it by my right hand.

"SNAKE!!!" I yelled.

Reacting instinctively, I rolled out into the bottom of the ditch. It rained harder. I quickly checked my hands for a snake bite. Then, ripping off my shirt and pants, I rubbed every part of my body to be sure the snake had not bitten me.

"ARTHUR!!!" I yelled louder.

All I heard was the sound of the soft rain. I checked again for swelling. None. I pulled my wet clothes over my body. Looking in the hole, I realized the snake was in hibernation. Carefully retrieving my gun, I shot it...several times...not to kill it deader than dead, but to relieve my frustration. Using a stick, I dragged it into the bottom of the ditch. The snake was approximately five feet long, and as fat as my wrist.

Arthur and I came back the next day looking for the snake, but some scavenger animal had dragged it off during the night.

There are many such dangers in the world, some known and others unknown. Some people won't walk through bushes because they are afraid of snakes. Some run when they see any snakes, poisonous or otherwise. Others pick up poisonous snakes. Others keep them as pets.

Some walk down a mountain path, not knowing how close they came to a disastrous fall. Others look at the steep rock cliff as a challenge to scale. They know it is dangerous, but they do not care. They live for thrills.

Living a Christian life is not a Sunday School picnic. There are dangers in your walk with Christ. There is an enemy that would destroy you; there is a possibility that you may fall. God, however, wants you to be a winner. He wants to help you avoid the dangers and temptations of life. This chapter describes what is implied when you pray, "Lead us not into temptation."

FIVE ESSENTIAL FACTS ABOUT TEMPTATION

1. God allows His children to be tempted
2. God's children can fall
3. God expects His children to overcome temptation
4. The Lord's Prayer can help you overcome temptation
5. There is a life of victory

When you ask God to "Lead us not into temptation," you are asking Him to guide your steps along a moral pathway. The previous petition, "Forgive us our debts," focused on *past* sins, while this petition, "Lead us not into temptation," focuses on *future* sins. The previous petition focused on actual sins; this petition focuses on potential sins—those that might happen, but in fact might not occur at all if God answers this prayer.

GOD ALLOWS HIS
CHILDREN TO BE TEMPTED

A minister once said in a sermon, "Opportunity knocks only once." He was talking about the good things that happen in your life.

Then he noted, "Temptation knocks the door down."

When you pray "Lead us not into temptation," you are recognizing that God is your Leader. You are confessing that you need a divine Leader, and you are asking God not to give up His leadership. You recognize that "The Lord is my shepherd;...he leadeth me" (Ps. 23:1,2). As a Shepherd, God leads you constantly: "He putteth forth his own sheep, he goeth before them, and the sheep follow him" (John 10:4).

When you pray "Lead us not into temptation," you are not praying, "Lord, don't tempt us." God would never tempt us, because He is good. God could never tempt us, because He is holy. "Let no man say when he is tempted, I am tempted of God: for God cannot be tempted with evil, neither tempteth he any man" (Jas. 1:13).

> God would not tempt us,
> because He is good.
> God could not tempt us,
> because He is holy.

When you pray "Lead me not into temptation," you are not praying, "Don't *allow* me to be tempted." That prayer denies the kind of world in which we live. Life is a test. We are like a little boy living in a world of many signs that say: *Wet Paint*. Our nature wants to touch them all.

This request, "Lead us not into temptation," is the cry of a heart that has experienced the devastation of sin. This prayer does not come out of our *heads*, which have correct knowledge of sin. It comes out of a *heart* that feels threatened by sin. We have felt the destruction of sin and we do not want to feel it again. This is a *heart prayer*, not a *head prayer*. Although this is not a precise theological statement, the heart prays, "I've been there, and I don't want to go there again."

Life is a test. God could have made us like the angels in heaven who do not sin. It would be useless for angels to pray "Lead us not into temptation," because they can't be tempted. They can't disobey God. They can only do good. Human beings, on the other hand, are free moral creatures who have the power of decision.

Life is not only a test, but it is also a choice. When we are tempted, we have a choice to resist or to give in. When a man thinks about looking at pornography, he has a choice to feed his lower nature or not to look. He can choose what he will think...what he will do....He has a choice to look or not look.

When a woman hears a juicy bit of gossip, she has a choice whether to ignore it or tantalize herself with little tidbits of information that destroy the reputation of another.

When a businessperson is faced with an illegal way of making a financial killing, he or she is faced with a choice.

When you pray "Lead us not into temptation," you are recognizing that life is a test that leads to a choice. Again, you are not praying, "God, don't tempt me." You are asking God not to lead you into a temptation that is too big for you. Because life is a test and choice, you will be tested. You are praying for victory: "Lord don't let me face a temptation that is too big to handle."

When you pray "Lead me not into temptation," it is like a husband saying to his wife, "Watch the road map and make sure I don't take a wrong turn." She would not intentionally get them lost. As we travel the roads of life, however, we take the wrong turns, we miss road signs and we get confused when we come to a complicated intersection.

When the man says to his wife, "Don't let me take the wrong turn," hopefully he is not fussing at her for past problems. Some husbands can't forget past mistakes. They constantly remind the wife, "Yesterday, we took a wrong turn; let's not do it again today." He is wrong because his wife would not automatically give wrong information to harm him.

So God would not lead us into temptation. Yet we are tempted. We have a rebellious nature, as when we like to stand closer to the edge than we should. A little child is playing when his ball rolls into the traffic. Obviously, the child is tempted to run get it. The child never sees danger and never thinks about getting hurt. The child just wants to retrieve his ball. A wise parent, though, sees danger and holds the child's hand to keep it from darting into the traffic. So we pray, "Lord, keep me from darting into traffic."

This prayer, "Lead us not into temptation," provides evidence of whether your conversion was genuine. When you have genuinely repented, it means you are truly sorry for past sins (see 2 Cor. 7:10,11). When you received Jesus Christ as your Savior, He forgave your sins, freeing you from guilt and punishment. Therefore, if you truly repented in the *first place,* it means you do not want to return to sin in the *second place.* So when you pray "Lead us not into temptation," you give evidence of repentance and conversion.

On the other hand, the person who continues to return to sin and has the attitude, "Because God has forgiven all sins, I don't have to worry about a thing," is giving evidence that he or she was not converted in the first place. We can question whether any Christian who continually goes back to the old way was genuinely saved (see 2 Pet. 2:22).

GOD'S CHILDREN CAN FALL

A minister once said in his sermon that you don't need to pray, "Lord...lead me not into temptation." When he said that, many wondered what he meant. Then the minister explained: "I can find temptation by myself."

When you pray "Lead us not into temptation," you are recognizing that people fall away from God. First, *internally* people are drawn away by their sinful nature. People have lust and desires that are contrary to God.

Every child is born both beauty and the beast. As beauty, the child has great desires to know and honor God in his or her life. Children are also a beast with a destructive nature that will destroy themselves, and everything they touch, or anything that touches them.

Why is it that one boy in a set of twins will become a great musician who lifts people up, and the other an alcoholic who destroys himself? Why will one twin girl become an unusual teacher, while the other becomes a prostitute?

Two forces dwell within every child, called the good nature and the evil nature (see Eph. 4:22-24). The child can give control to either nature, and that choice of natures will determine the destiny of the child. There is in each of us a Dr. Jekyll, which has an *internal* attraction to destruction; and a Mr. Hyde, which has an *external* attraction to do God's will.

Satan will set a trap for every believer, a specific temptation to trip up a person. That trap will be aimed at the weakness of the person. When you pray "Lead us not into temptation," you are asking God not to lead you into that trap.

John calls that trap "the world":

Love not the world [the world system], neither the things that are in the world....For all that is in the world, the lust of the flesh, and the lust of the eyes, and the pride of life, is not of the Father, but is of the world (1 John 2:15,16).

The world that will trap you is not a physical or geographical place. Your "trap" is not the world of purple mountains, trees, oceans and plains. The world that is a trap is a system of ideas, experiences and energy. The world that is a trap is like the world of rock and roll music that influences the way people think and experience, and produces its own lifestyle. The same could be said about the world of classical music, or of stock-car racing. When the Bible says "Love not the world," it is describing anti-God thinking, anti-God experiences and living contrary to God's design.

John says that the world that is a trap is made up of three things. First there is the "lust of the flesh," which means the desires of the flesh. This could include laziness, wrongly satisfying sexual appetites or a host of addictions. God wants our bodies free to serve Him.

Second, there is the "lust of the eyes"—desiring things that are not ours (i.e., stealing, coveting, lying about possessions, etc.).

"The pride of life" is the third aspect of the worldly trap. This involves putting self on the throne of our lives. Although nothing is wrong with pride that is self-respect, the Bible condemns pride that exalts itself against God and refuses to accept His standards.

When people reject the Ten Commandments, they usually reject God's rule over their lives because they want to fulfill their own desires (lust of the flesh). They want to live their own lifestyles rather than God's (lust of the eyes), and they think their ideas of how to live are better than God's (pride of life).

When you pray "Lead us not into temptation," you are saying, Don't lead me into the world trap that would harm me. You are asking for a life of victory. When God answers this prayer, you can say with Paul, "Thanks be unto God who giveth us the victory in Christ" (2 Cor. 2:14, author's translation).

When you pray "Lead us not into temptation," you give evidence of a changed attitude toward sin. We are not saying you will never sin again after you become a Christian. Remember, the Bible recognizes that all will fall into sin: "If we say that we have no sin [sin nature], we deceive ourselves" (1 John 1:8). Beyond our sin nature, "If we say that we have not sinned [continual acts of sin], we make him a liar, and his word is not in us" (v. 10). So we may inadvertently trip and fall into sin.

Christ gives the sincerely converted a new *attitude*. He wants us to live by a new *goal*. He wants us to aim at perfection, although He realizes that we live in world where no one is perfect. Even imperfect people can aim high. This is what John meant when he said, "Whosoever is born of God sinneth not [continually]" (5:18).

When you pray "Lead us not into temptation," you recognize the tyranny of sin. When you sin, it is not the same as a baby who spills a cup of milk. That is only a mistake, and we all make mistakes. Sin is rebellion against God and His standards. Mistakes like spilled milk can ruin carpets, tablecloths or even clothing. That just costs us money.

Sin is internal, though, and has far deeper influences in our lives. Sin is a tyrannical master that tyrannizes us. Sin makes us addicts to alcohol or sex. Sin puts us into bondage to drugs. Sin destroys our self-respect, and puts us into prison. Sin makes us lose our tempers, so we lose our friends, our jobs, our marriages.

When you pray "Lead us not into temptation," you recognize what sin can do to you and you tell God you do not want to go back into its bondage.

GOD EXPECTS HIS CHILDREN TO OVERCOME TEMPTATION

When you are tempted to sin, you face the greatest test of life. This test is greater than any final exam in college, greater than any bar exam faced by a lawyer, greater than any certification test faced by a professional. Temptation is a test to determine if you will be faithful to God or deny Him. This test will establish your character. Satan wants to destroy your virtue.

So why should we pray, "Lead us not into temptation"? Because temptation gets to us at the point of what our lower nature wants. We want to be happy, satisfied and fulfilled. We think that sin will make us happy, satisfy us and fulfill us. James noted, "Every man is tempted, when he is drawn away of his own lust, and enticed" (Jas. 1:14). So when Jesus told us to pray "Lead us not into temptation," He was giving us a key to overcome our sinful nature, recognizing that we have a bent to wander from God.

When you pray "Lead us not into temptation," you are asking for God to keep you from sin. Jude expressed this possibility: "Now unto him that is able to keep you from falling" (Jude 24). You need to know that God expects you not to sin, He can keep you from sin, and you can live victoriously. To be victorious is not the same as living sinlessly. Remember, when the Bible promises that God can "keep you from falling," it is affirming the possibility that God can keep you from sinning to avoid a fall.

When you pray "Lead us not into temptation," you are asking for sanctification. The word "sanctify" means to set apart or make holy. On behalf of the Thessalonians, Paul prayed that "the very God of peace sanctify you wholly" (1 Thess. 5:23). Because the word "sanctify" means "to set apart," when you are sanctified to God you are set apart from the world to glorify Him and live for Him. So when you pray "Lead us not into temptation," you are asking for God to set you apart to His glory and to live for Him.

THE LORD'S PRAYER CAN HELP YOU OVERCOME TEMPTATION

When you pray "Lead us not into temptation," you are establishing a watchful attitude over your spiritual life. This is the same prayer Jesus gave to His disciples in the garden after He found them sleeping: "Watch and pray, that ye enter not into temptation: the spirit indeed is willing, but the flesh is weak" (Matt. 26:41).

When you pray "Lead us not into temptation," you are asking for deliverance from both a crisis and a process. In referring to temptation, Jesus used the word *peirasmos*, which implies that temptation is a process. This means, Don't put me into a place of seduction where I wrestle with temptation every day.

When a football team beats its cross-town rival, it does not have to beat them every day to be the best team. They schedule one game a year, and the winner is the best team. So when we pray the Lord's Prayer in the face of temptation, we are praying, "Don't allow us to be continually tempted by a particular sin."

Life itself is a process. When we gain victory over one sin, another temptation always seems to be waiting to trip us up. Therefore, praying "Lead me not into temptation" is an appeal for God to enable us to go "from victory to victory." We are praying, "Lord, give me a victory today"; and tomorrow you will pray again, "Lord, give me a victory today."

When you pray "Lead us not into temptation," you are also asking for deliverance in a crisis. Perhaps you have never been tempted to steal. Suppose, though, you had the opportunity to walk away with a million dollars...no one would know...absolutely no one would know...positively no way of getting caught. All you have to do is say a simple yes. When you pray "Lead us not into temptation," you are asking for deliverance from a massive crisis that would destroy your soul. You are asking for the courage to say no in a crisis.

When you pray "Lead us not into temptation," you are like a night watchman who discovers a blazing inferno in the warehouse. He does not try to fight the fire himself, but runs to call the fire department to fight the fire. You also call for God's help to face your own fires of temptation.

When you pray "Lead us not into temptation," you might want to add, "Help me to run as fast as I can to get away from temptation." For some reason, the word "lead" implies a slow walk. Because you have been there before, however, you know how dangerous tempting situations are. Paul told Timothy, "Flee these things" (1 Tim. 6:11). Obviously, the word "flee" means to dash, as a person would race away from a burning car before the fuel tank explodes.

When you pray "Lead us not into temptation," you are claiming victory in the spirit of 1 Corinthians 10:13:

> There hath no temptation taken you but such as is common to man: but God is faithful, who will not suffer you

to be tempted above that ye are able; but will with the temptation also make a way to escape, that ye may be able to bear it.

In praying the Lord's Prayer, you are asking for God to lead you to a place where you can overcome temptation, just as He promised to do.

When you pray "Lead us not into temptation," you recognize that if you boastfully think you can stand against temptation, you will fall. Paul warns the believer, "Wherefore let him that thinketh he standeth take heed lest he fall" (1 Cor. 10:12).

When you pray "Lead us not into temptation," you exercise the humility of self-distrust. You know that in yourself you can fall, so you ask God to lead you away from temptation so you won't fall.

Because you don't trust your mouth, you take precautions about what you say (see Rom. 3:13). Because you don't trust your feet, you take precautions where you go, (see v. 15). Because you don't trust your eyes, you take precautions what you see (see v. 18). Because you don't trust your mind, you take precautions what you read (see v. 11). Because you don't trust your heart, you take precautions with your desires (see Matt. 15:17-20; Jer. 17:9).

When you pray "Lead us not into temptation," you are also asking God to keep you from the place of temptation. For the word "into" here, Jesus used the Greek preposition *eis*. We pray, "Don't lead me *into* temptation."

The Lord could have used many other prepositions. He could have used *en*, and the prayer would mean, "Don't lead us in the very middle of temptation." He could have used the preposition *epi*, which would mean, "Don't lead us around the edge of temptation." That would mean that we could come near to temptation, but walk around it.

The Lord could have used the preposition *para*, which would mean, "Don't lead us around the outside of temptation." This is illustrated by a person walking around a house. Or the Lord could have used the preposition *dia*, which would mean, "Don't lead us through the middle of temptation." That would be leading us into and out of temptation. However, the Lord said to pray, "Do not lead us *eis* temptation," which means, "Lead us not *into* temptation's influence, with its purpose of sin reaching or touching us."

THERE IS A LIFE OF VICTORY

When you pray "Lead us not into temptation," you are recognizing the leadership of God in giving you victory in a moral test. Sometimes, that test will come to you as a young Christian. What may seem insurmountable, with God's help can be overcome. Later on in life, that same test returns to us, and this time it does not faze us. That temptation is a toothless paper tiger. That test is no longer suited to our spiritual maturity, so it means nothing.

Put that shoe on the other foot. A test that is suited to your spiritual maturity later in life may have destroyed you as a young believer had you not prayed, "Lead me not into temptation."

God is like a school teacher. In the first grade you were tested to see if you could print letters. In the middle grades, you were tested to see if you could write sentences, paragraphs, even a short paper. By the time you got to college, you should have been able to write a term paper, supporting your arguments by using quotations from authorities. So a teacher tests the college student on college material, not on first-grade material.

In the same way, "Lead us not into temptation" is a way of praying, "Lead us only into temptations that we are able to withstand." A loving God, like a conscientious teacher, gives tests we are able to pass.

God also controls the amount of temptation when we pray, "Lead us not into temptation." When you are a young Christian, you perhaps can only handle one temptation at a time. As you become older, you can handle many temptations at once. The beginning golfer only works at one aspect of his game at a time. He works on driving, chipping or putting. Later, as a mature golfer, he is working on his grip, stance, swing and rhythm, all at the same time. Our heavenly Father does not put more on us than we can withstand.

The night before Jesus died He prayed, "I pray not that thou shouldest take them out of the world, but that thou shouldest keep them from the evil" (John 17:15). When you pray "Lead us not into temptation," you are praying the same prayer Jesus prayed in His High Priestly Prayer.

PRAYER CHECKLIST

Lead us not into temptation *List areas in which you want victory.*	How are you doing? (check one)		
	Lousy	*Average*	*Great*
1.			
2.			
3.			
4.			
5.			
6.			
7.			

JOURNALING

Keeping a journal is a serious attempt to grow as a Christian. You write down your impressions so you can learn from them later. Here you will want to write down your struggles with temptations. Just keeping a record of when you fall will not necessarily strengthen you. Keep a record of your experiences, both positive and negative.

1. Write down the things you have done to overcome temptation. Include your prayers, your Bible reading and anything else you did to be victorious.
2. Try to describe how you felt when you were victorious over sin and what that feeling did for you. Were any Bible verses meaningful to you in enabling you to enjoy your victorious experience?
3. What happened to you as you prayed the Lord's Prayer? How was it effective in your life?

THREE-STEP BIBLE STUDY

FACING AND OVERCOMING TEMPTATION

This Bible study will help you understand the things that trip you up in your Christian life. Remember: Step 1—Read the question to understand the problems you face. Step 2—Read the Bible verses to understand what God says about the topic, trying to apply the meaning of each verse to your life. Step 3—Write your answers in the spaces provided.

1. Where does sin enter your life?

> "Therefore to him that knoweth to do good, and doeth it not, to him it is sin."—James 4:17

_____

_____

_____

_____

2. Who is your role model when you are tempted?

> "For we have not an high priest which cannot be touched with the feeling of our infirmities; but was in all points tempted like as we are, yet without sin."—Hebrews 4:15

_____

_____

_____

3. How did Jesus overcome temptation?

> "Then was Jesus led up of the spirit into the wilderness to be tempted of the devil."—Matthew 4:1
> "But he [Jesus] answered and said, It is written, Man shall not live by bread alone, but by every word that proceedeth out of the mouth of God."—Matthew 4:4

_____
_____
_____
_____

4. What is an inner secret to your victory over temptation?

"Thy word have I hid in mine heart, that I might not sin against thee."—Psalm 119:11

_____
_____
_____
_____

5. What attitude can you assume to protect yourself from temptation?

"To put off your old self, which is being corrupted by its deceitful desires; to be made new in the attitude of your minds; and to put on the new self, created to be like God in true righteousness and holiness."—Ephesians 4:22-24 (NIV)

_____
_____
_____
_____

6. What is an outer response to temptation?

"Submit yourselves therefore to God. Resist the devil, and he will flee from you."—James 4:7

_____
_____
_____
_____

7. What is God's promise to you when tempted?

"There hath no temptation taken you but such as is common to man: but God is faithful, who will not suffer you to be tempted above that ye are able; but will with the temptation also make a way to escape, that ye may be able to bear it."—1 Corinthians 10:13

_____

_____

_____

8. What is the reward to those who successfully overcome temptation?

"Blessed is the man that endureth temptation: for when he is tried, he shall receive the crown of life, which the Lord hath promised to them that love him."—James 1:12

_____

_____

_____

Martin Luther's Morning Prayer

_⟨⟩_

We give thanks to thee, Heavenly Father, through Jesus
Christ, thy dear Son, that thou hast protected us through
the night from all danger and harm; and we beseech thee
to preserve and keep us, this day also, from all sin and
evil, that in all our thoughts, words, and deeds, we may
serve and please thee, into thy hands we commend our
bodies and souls; and all that is ours. Let thy holy angel
have charge concerning us, that the Wicked One have no
power over us. Amen.

— ❧ 10 ❧ —

THE SEVENTH
PETITION:
DELIVER US FROM EVIL

Protection for My Life

In the summer of 1995, I was asked to deliver a message at a Nazarene encampment near Springfield, Illinois. After arriving at the campground, I was asked to present an additional message because a denominational official had not arrived. He was traveling to the same camp with his wife on the same Interstate highway I had been on, but he had an unusual accident, which can't be explained naturally. A lug bolt came off a speeding tractor-trailer truck tire with such force that it came through the windshield like a rifle bullet.

My husband's been shot, his wife thought as she wrestled the car to a stop.

The man's chest was punctured like a rifle wound. In a world where Ripley's truth is stranger than fiction, that bolt could have hit or missed the man. I could have been on the highway when the lug bolt came loose, and it could have hit me instead of the scheduled speaker. It could have killed me. He could have been taking my place. (The man lived.) That morning I had prayed the Lord's Prayer, meditating on the petition,

"Deliver us from the evil one."

I once conducted a seminar at a Holiday Inn in Hollywood, California. About 150 people were present in the conference room. We had discussed the work of God, and the day had gone well. I knew many of the conference participants would come up to ask me to pray with them individually. Instead of a benediction, which would have closed the meeting, I told them I wanted to dedicate them to God's service. I asked all to kneel by their chairs for a closing prayer of dedication. For some reason, instead of praying near the center of the room where I had been standing, I walked over to the end chair on the first row near the window and knelt down.

After offering a prayer of dedication for the seminar delegates, I concluded my prayer with the Lord's Prayer. I did not pray it word for word as some churches do on Sunday morning. Instead, I paraphrased the words of the Lord's Prayer, applying it to the audience. When I came to the last petition, I prayed:

"Deliver us from the evil one who would harm us in a traffic accident on the way home. Deliver us from the evil one who would destroy our health by disease or germs. Deliver us from the evil one who would hurt us in ways we don't even think about."

When I concluded my prayer, I stood up and walked away from the window toward the lectern. Suddenly, as I was walking from the spot, the entire window frame fell out of the casing, crashing onto the chair I had just left. Shattered glass flew in every direction.

The audience yelled.

No one was hurt by the glass. The heavy ornate Spanish window frame was smashed over the chair where I had just knelt. I do not think it was heavy enough to have killed me. I have no idea, though, what would have happened to me if I had not moved.

Most of those present said they believed God protected me because of the Lord's Prayer I had just prayed. Because Satan is trying to destroy everyone belonging to God, all of us should pray daily the Lord's Prayer for God's protection. Because we do not know what dangers we will face each new day, we need God's protective blanket to cover us.

"A verse a day, keeps the devil away" is an old Sunday School slogan that sounds nice to children. It may take more than just reading a Bible verse every day to be protected from danger.

The traditional *King James Version* of the Bible reads, "Deliver us from evil," and the *New King James Version* reads, "Deliver us from the evil one." When you pray "Deliver us from the evil one," you are confessing that you believe there is a supremely evil one who will harm you. This suggests that the Christian life is more than attending worship, or more than adopting the power of positive thinking. When you use the phrase "Deliver us from the evil one," you are admitting that this life is a struggle with an enemy who opposes you. Therefore, this chapter is about warfare...fighting...combat...winning...or losing.

When you pray "Deliver us from the evil one," you confess your belief in four essential facts about your enemy, the devil. When you know how to pray the Lord's Prayer, you can successfully fight the enemy. You can protect yourself from defeat, and win the battle for control of your soul.

FOUR ESSENTIAL FACTS ABOUT THE EVIL ONE

1. The evil one exists
2. The evil one is in conflict with you
3. God is your deliverer
4. You can use the Lord's Prayer for deliverance

Every new soldier goes through basic training, sometimes called "boot camp." In boot camp, a new soldier learns how to fight the enemy. Mastering the first three petitions of the Lord's Prayer is similar to learning the initial lessons of boot camp, for they teach you the basic focus of the Christian life.

First, you learn to worship God (i.e., "Hallowed be Thy name").

Second, you learn to obey the King's principles: "Thy kingdom come."

Third, you submit to orders: "Thy will be done."

Next, as a new soldier, you receive nutrition for combat by asking for necessities: "Give us daily bread."

The final three petitions take us into conflict with our enemy. In the fifth petition you receive forgiveness of sin when you pray, "Forgive us our debts." The sixth petition gives you victory over defeat when you pray, "Lead us not into temptation." The last petition gives you protection when you pray, "Deliver us from the evil one."

THE EVIL ONE EXISTS

The Christian life is not a Sunday School picnic where you play games and drink Kool-Aid. We have an enemy who tries relentlessly to destroy us. Life is a battlefield between competitive forces. Because the enemy hates God, he hates us and fights against us.

Paul understood that when believers give in to sin, they become tools of Satan. It is the enemy's way of hurting God's work and ultimately hurting God. Paul told the Corinthians,

> The people you forgave for sinning against your church, I forgive; because Satan gets to us if we have an unforgiving spirit. I forgive them because I live in Christ. I am not ignorant of Satan's devices to get to me (2 Cor. 2:10,11, author's translation).

```
When Satan gets to us,
he gets to God.
```

Week after week, a man stood up to pray at his church's prayer meeting. Typically, he closed his prayer with the phrase, "Clean all the cobwebs out of my life."

After listening to this man's continual request, the night came when a friend blurted out in prayer, "Lord, kill the spider instead!"

How often do we find ourselves confronting the "cobwebs" while ignoring the "spider" in our lives? Our main adversary is greater than a spider; it is the evil one. At boot camp, new soldiers learn who their enemies are and how the enemy will attack them. In the same way, children of God need to know about their enemy.

The problem is that we live in a culture filled with fairy tales or false information about the evil one. If we were to ask a dozen different people what they thought about Satan, we might get a dozen different answers.

During the Middle Ages, people enjoyed religious plays for entertainment. Through the years, the devil was played by actors who were dressed in red suits, showing horns and carrying pitchforks. Even today people think the devil is evil looking. When portrayed in movies, he has a sinister appearance.

Because of the recent increased interest in the occult, Satan has become a box office attraction at the movies. We also see a growing cult of Satan worshipers. People are prepared to give Satan control over their lives to a greater or lesser degree. The interest and influence of Satan is growing from simple things such as movies and certain teenage music videos to more serious things such as witches' covens and stores that sell artifacts relating to satanism.

Another group denies the existence of Satan completely. Someone noted that if you take the *d* out of "devil," you make it "evil," and that there is no personification of evil. Certain factions deny the supernatural aspect of the devil; others recognize his existence but deny his power. Because deceit is one of the characteristics of Satan, it is understandable why so many Christians are deceived concerning his nature and work. Satan has blinded people about it. He is effective when he keeps himself hidden from public sight.

The evil one has many names. John described him thus: "The great dragon...that old serpent, called the Devil, and Satan, which deceiveth the whole world" (Rev. 12:9). Jesus called him, "A murderer...a liar, and the father of it" (John 8:44).

THE EVIL ONE IS IN CONFLICT WITH YOU

Years ago, an artist painted a portrait of the devil playing against a young man in a game of chess. The painting hung in an art museum in Cincinnati, Ohio. The story about the painting claimed that the devil had challenged a young chess player to a game. If the young man won, he would be eternally free from the influence of evil. If he lost, the devil would possess his soul. The picture showed the devil's determination to win. Chess experts who saw the picture realized that in just four short moves the young man would lose. The picture portrays torment in the face of the man as the devil is moving his queen to announce checkmate. The young man has his hand over his rook, amazed and disheartened at what appears to be his ultimate loss.

For years the picture in the Cincinnati art gallery communicated doom and despondency. As viewers passed the portrait, they saw the hopelessness of the young man's situation. Some of the world's finest chess players stood amazed at the artist's brilliance in chess playing and its application to life.

Finally, one person who studied the picture was convinced someone could beat the devil in a chess game. He arranged for an aging chess master, Paul Murphy, to come from New York to study the picture. A crowd gathered to see if the chess master could solve the dilemma. He sat attempting moves, only to see the futility of those attempts. Then suddenly the old man's eyes lit up as he realized there was an unthought-of combination of moves. As he made the moves, they not only saved the young man's king, but also placed the devil in checkmate. When he explained the solution, the people shouted, "Young man, make that move!"

Many Christians believe they can do nothing but surrender to the evil one if he attacks them. Others are terrorized by thoughts of the devil's influence on them. The Bible, on the other hand, claims, "Greater is he that is in you, than he that is in the world" (1 John 4:4).

All of Satan's works are against God. The very meaning of the name Satan is "adversary." At times, he actively opposes the work or plan of God. On other occasions, he simply imitates God to draw Christians away from His simple plan to save them.

When you pray "Deliver us from the evil one," you are turning your protection over to God. You are not giving in to the threats of your opponent. You have refused to live in fear of the evil one. You ask God to shield your life.

GOD IS YOUR DELIVERER

It should be more natural for us to defeat Satan than for him to defeat us. God has revealed certain principles in His Word that can protect the Christian against defeat. More than insulating us against evil, though, these principles can make us victorious over the evil one. The Bible clearly states:

> There hath no temptation taken you but such as is common to man: but God is faithful, who will not suffer you

to be tempted above that ye are able; but will with the temptation also make a way to escape, that ye may be able to bear it (1 Cor. 10:13).

That "way to escape" is found by applying biblical principles to each temptation.

YOU CAN USE THE LORD'S PRAYER FOR DELIVERANCE

The Principle of Respect

Too often Christians rely on fleshly strength to deliver them from Satan. Though Jesus is greater than the devil (see 1 John 4:4), we must still have a healthy respect for our enemy. If a good football team becomes overconfident, it may lose to a lesser team. Overconfidence will cause a team to play carelessly, allowing the opposition to do things it could not otherwise accomplish.

A master outdoorsman is not afraid of a poisonous rattlesnake, but he will respect the snake and not put himself in danger. He knows how to treat the snake and how to avoid being bitten. We do not fear the evil one because we are to fear only God (see Deut. 31:12). It is God who holds our destiny in His hands. We respect the evil one's craftiness and guile enough to avoid him, though.

The Principle of Removal

It has often been said that one bad apple will spoil the whole barrel. This principle also applies to a confrontation with the devil. Wise Christians should evaluate their lives and avoid those areas where they are most likely to be tempted. Paul reminds us, "Abstain from all appearance of evil" (1 Thess. 5:22). He also says, "Flee these [evil] things" (1 Tim. 6:11).

A little boy met his father at the front door and announced to the proud dad,

"I beat a snake today...."

The father was surprised at his son's boldness, and that he knew how to rid the yard of snakes. So he asked his son,

"Did you beat the snake with a stick or a rock?"

"I beat him running..." the lad explained.

You should not attempt to attack the evil one, nor enter into conflict with the evil forces. A few specialists know how to confront the evil one in spiritual warfare, but the average child of God should not do it without training and wisdom.

The Principle of Resistance
A Christian is disobedient if he or she passively entertains Satan or his influence. James counsels, "Submit yourselves therefore to God. Resist the devil, and he will flee from you" (Jas. 4:7). It is possible for God's children to protect themselves from the evil one by taking definite actions.

The apostle Peter advised believers that they should not give in to Satan, but "resist stedfast in the faith" (1 Pet. 5:9). We will not be defeated if we will quote the name of Jesus Christ and refuse to listen to temptation from the evil one. When Jesus was tempted, He resisted the devil by using the Scriptures, and thus gained the victory (see Matt. 4:1-11).

The Principle of Readiness
The Boy Scouts have the motto, "Be prepared." That principle should be the watchword of the tempted Christian. Jesus said, "Watch ye and pray, lest ye enter into temptation" (Mark 14:38). Paul advised the Ephesians, "Put on the whole armour of God, that ye may be able to stand against the wiles of the devil" (Eph. 6:11). Prepared Christians will recognize their weak areas and strengthen them.

OUR STRATEGY
Respect our enemy.
Remove from evil.
Resist danger.
Stay ready.

When you pray "Deliver us from the evil one," you have made a decision to let God protect you. That decision does two things for you. First, it empowers your will to obey God. When you decide to ask God's help, you put yourself on His side against the evil one.

> You don't have the *power* to obey,
> until you make a *decision* to obey.

Second, when you decide to let God protect you from the evil one, you bring God into your experience. God is wiser than you, and He knows how to defend you. God is more powerful than you, and He has the power to defend you. The psalmist had this confidence: "The Lord shall preserve thee from all evil:...The Lord shall preserve thy going out and thy coming in" (Ps. 121:7,8).

PRAYER CHECKLIST

Deliver us from the evil one *List those for whom you pray.*	How are you doing? (check one)		
	Lousy	*Average*	*Great*
1.			
2.			
3.			
4.			
5.			
6.			
7.			

JOURNALING

Each day you should ask God for spiritual protection for yourself and others around you. Make a list of those for whom you pray. Note also the ways you think God has answered by protecting you.

1. What are the areas in which you need protection? Usually your "track record" is a good way to determine how the enemy has attacked you. How you have been attacked in the past can serve to predict future problems. When you write these out, you become more aware of where you need protection in the future.
2. Relate how God has delivered you or protected you. This can be spiritual, intellectual, psychological, social or physical.
3. Describe how some days your prayers for protection are more intense than others.
4. What does praying "Deliver us from the evil one" do to your feelings? Confidence? Fears?

THREE-STEP BIBLE STUDY

PROTECTION FROM THE EVIL ONE

This lesson will show you how God protects His children from harm. Step 1—Read the question to understand the problem that faces you. Step 2—Read the Bible verse to understand what God says about the issue, then try to apply the answer to your life. Step 3—Write your answer in the space provided.

1. Who seeks to harm Christians?

> "Be sober, be vigilant; because your adversary the devil, as a roaring lion, walketh about, seeking whom he may devour."—1 Peter 5:8

_____
_____
_____
_____

2. How does the enemy attack non-Christians?

"Then cometh the devil, and taketh away the word out of their hearts, lest they should believe and be saved."
—Luke 8:12

_____

_____

_____

_____

3. What else does the enemy do to non-Christians?

"The god of this world hath blinded the minds of them which believe not, lest the light of the glorious gospel of Christ, who is the image of God, should shine unto them."—2 Corinthians 4:4

_____

_____

_____

4. How would Satan trick you?

"False apostles,...transforming themselves into the apostles of Christ. And no marvel; for Satan himself is transformed into an angel of light. Therefore it is no great thing if his ministers also be transformed as the ministers of righteousness."—2 Corinthians 11:13-15

_____

_____

_____

_____

5. What else would the enemy do to you and how will God help you?

"And the Lord said, Simon, Simon, behold, Satan hath desired to have you, that he may sift you as wheat: but I have prayed for thee, that thy faith fail not."
—Luke 22:31,32

6. What should be your attitude toward the attacks of the enemy?

"Put on the whole armour of God, that ye may be able to stand against the wiles of the devil. For we wrestle not against flesh and blood, but against principalities, against powers, against the rulers of the darkness of this world, against spiritual wickedness in high places."
—Ephesians 6:11,12

7. What promise do believers have as they face their enemy, the evil one?

"Ye are of God, little children, and have overcome them: because greater is he that is in you, than he that is in the world."—1 John 4:4

8. What promises will encourage you?

> "The Lord shall preserve thee from all evil: he shall preserve thy soul. The Lord shall preserve thy going out and thy coming in from this time forth, and even for evermore."—Psalm 121:7,8

_____

_____

_____

_____

Controlling the Lord's Prayer

What discord you would introduce into this world if God answered all your prayers! For then you—not God—would control the world. So when God does not answer all your prayers, maybe He is just reminding you who is in control.

～๑ II ๑～

THE BENEDICTION:
HOW TO FINISH RIGHT

When you finish your prayer with the benediction, "For thine is the kingdom, and the power, and the glory," you are making three positive statements to God. These statements can become positive attitudes that can change your life, and lead to a greater life of prayer.

THE ESSENTIAL FACTS ABOUT
GOD FROM THE BENEDICTION

Kingdom: God's right to answer prayer in His way
Power: God's ability to give you what you ask
Glory: God's credit for your blessings

FOR THINE IS THE KINGDOM

When you pray "For thine is the kingdom," you have finished the seven petitions and you are entering the benediction to the Lord's Prayer. You are wrapping up your prayer to God.

When making a business sale, it is important how you begin *and* how you finish. The success of the sales presentation is getting the order. The success of any prayer is twofold: glorifying God, and receiving an answer from Him.

Because you pray "Thine is the kingdom," you recognize God's rule over your life.

Because you pray "Thine is the kingdom," you recognize God is the sovereign ruler of the earth and of your life.

Because you pray "Thine is the kingdom," you acknowledge that God is the source of answered prayers.

Because you pray "Thine is the kingdom," you recognize that God has the right to refuse your request.

Because you pray "Thine is the kingdom," you recognize that God can and will answer your prayers the way He chooses.

When you acknowledge "Thine is the kingdom," you are telling God that He is the King over your life and you are submitting to be a follower in His kingdom.

FOR THINE IS THE POWER

When you conclude your prayer by saying the phrase "Thine is the power," you are acknowledging God's awesome ability to answer your prayers.

Because you pray "Thine is the power," you recognize that you are God's servant and He is your Boss.

Because you pray "Thine is the power," you yield yourself to whatever answer God chooses to send.

Because you pray "Thine is the power," you recognize God is the Creator and Ruler of this world.

Because you pray "Thine is the power," you recognize that people were made in God's image and are accountable to His natural and supernatural laws.

Because you pray "Thine is the kingdom," you recognize God's control over your life, including its pain and its pleasure.

Because you pray "Thine is the power," you recognize God's sovereignty to do what He desires, when He wants to do it, the way He sees fit.

When you acknowledge "Thine is the power," you realize that God *may* give you what you ask if it is His will. You also recognize that He *will* not answer when it is contrary to His laws and purpose.

He *may* wait because the timing is wrong. God will never turn you down because He can't do what you ask, however, unless you ask Him to do something wrong or contrary to His nature. For example, you can never ask God to make a lie into the truth, or to make 2 plus 2 equal 3 or to make a rock too big for Him to lift.

When you acknowledge "Thine is the power," you are telling God to answer according to His omnipotent ability. God may perform a miracle to answer your request, transcending or suspending the laws by which He ordinarily governs the world.

God may answer by changing the internal attitude of people. Jacob wrestled with God all night in prayer because he was afraid his brother would kill him. God answered by changing the pent-up anger his brother Esau had stored up for 20 years. God may answer in any number of ways; but no matter how He answers, our response can only be, "Thine is the power."

For Thine Is the Glory

When you pray "Thine is the glory," you recognize that God must get credit for all our answers to prayer, all we are, all we have and all we do.

Because you pray "Thine is the glory," you confess that any answers you receive will not be because of your intercessory ability or because there is anything good in you.

Because you pray "Thine is the glory," you confess that God gets all the credit for any answers that come.

Because you pray "Thine is the glory," you reject any credit that comes to you for correctly praying the Lord's Prayer, or because you prayed daily the Lord's Prayer.

Some people want a reputation as an intercessor with God. Others want to be known for their great faith, or their godly piety. "The heart is deceitful" (Jer. 17:9), so some pray to the King of heaven for answers, but they want to be known as "King makers." They want to make God do what they ask. They treat God like a dog who fetches a stick, and then they take credit for having such a wonderful "stick fetcher."

When you pray "Thine is the glory," you must completely take your hands off the request. You must let God do it in His own way, and whatever the answer, all credit goes to Him.

THE BENEDICTION

When you properly finish the Lord's Prayer using the benediction that Jesus gave, you will have three responses from your heart.

THREE ESSENTIALS AFTER PRAYING THE LORD'S PRAYER

1. *Faith:* to believe God will answer
2. *Hope:* that your future will be bright
3. *Praise:* that God receives your worship

FAITH:
TO BELIEVE GOD WILL ANSWER

Your prayer "Thine is the kingdom" is a statement that God rules the world, and therefore expresses your faith that He has a strategy to answer your request. You are looking to God's principles to accomplish your prayer. Because faith is trust in God, you conclude your prayer with this expression of trust in Him to give you what you need, when you need it, the way you need it.

Your prayer "Thine is the kingdom" is an expression of God's ability to grant your request. Many people believe in God, and know He has worked in the past. However, they are not sure He can do anything now. They close their eyes to pray, but peek to see how He is doing, or to see if He is doing anything at all. They always want to help God, as though He is not able to answer by Himself. When you conclude "Thine is the power," however, you are telling God that you believe He is able to do it by Himself.

You also make a faith statement when you pray, "Thine is the glory." You are affirming that the answers to your prayers are coming, so you are praising God for them before they appear. It is like a little child who asks, "May I have some cookies?"—then says, "Thank-you" before the cookies are given. When you pray "Thine is the glory," you are telling God "Thank-you" for the answer before it comes.

HOPE:
THAT YOUR FUTURE WILL BE BRIGHT

"Thine is the kingdom" is a "hope builder." Your prayer should build up hope...hope in God...hope in your calling...hope in God's work ...hope in the future.

Hope is a healing medicine for depressed believers. Hope is soul aspirin for those who suffer from chronic discouragement.

When you pray "Thine is the kingdom," you express hope in God's reign and rule. You are telling God that you "know that all things work together for good to them that love God" (Rom. 8:28).

Your hope also grows when you honestly pray, "Thine is the power." You are not looking for answers that flow from your ability, but from God's. When a football team is struggling against a stronger team, the players often lose hope. Along with loss of hope comes poor play execution and poor performance. So when a football team lacks hope, it usually gets its brains beat out.

Just one prayer can make a difference, though. A team becomes recharged with hope when it sees a big tackle coming back in after an injury, or a quarterback who has previously led them to victory coming into the game. Someone who has more strength than the hopeless players can ignite hope, often causing players to play above their heads and achieve beyond their ordinary ability.

When you honestly tell God "Thine is the power," you are renewing your hope not only in God, but also in yourself. Having revived hope you will work harder, achieve more and win spiritual victories beyond your ability. Then just think of what God can and will do. Hope releases your faith and ability, and releases God to do God-sized exploits.

Paul tells us, "We are labourers together with God" (1 Cor. 3:9). David tells us, "Through God we shall do valiantly: for he it is that shall tread down our enemies" (Ps. 60:12). That Psalm was David's prayer for strength to defeat the giant Goliath.

The spontaneous expression of hope will bring glory to God because it is like a child in trouble expressing infinite confidence in his or her father to fix things. Your expectant attitude therefore magnifies God. Remember that when you magnify God, you do not make Him bigger or better. Your worship is like putting on reading glasses.

Your glasses do not make the letters larger on the paper, but only in your eyes and mind. When you magnify God, you see Him "bigger," so you understand things better.

PRAISE:
THAT GOD RECEIVES YOUR WORSHIP

You end the Lord's Prayer as you began it...with praise and worship. Remember, when you worship God, no matter where you are...He will come to receive your praise. The psalmist said of God, "Thou art holy, O thou that inhabitest the praises of Israel" (Ps. 22:3).

In the movie *Field of Dreams*, the farmer was told, "If you build it, they will come." When you worship God, you can be sure He will come to receive your praise. You end the Lord's Prayer in His presence just as you began it. God did not get bored and drift off to sleep. He did not get busy and turn His attention elsewhere, nor did He wander off to leave you talking to the ceiling. He is there.

FOR EVER AND EVER

"For ever" is a wonderful thought for ending your worship. Actually, you are praying "Thine is the kingdom...for ever." This affirms that God's kingdom principles will not change, nor will they be canceled for bad weather as might a plane reservation.

When you pray "Thine is the power...for ever," you know that God's ability today will not be short-circuited by a power shortage.

The phrase "Thine is the glory...for ever," reminds us that when our prayers are answered it is of God's will, by God's power and for God's glory.

When you say "for ever" at the end of the Lord's Prayer, you recognize God's eternality. God existed from the beginning and will never end. The Bible says, "In the beginning God..." and nothing ends without God. He is for ever and ever.

When you confess that God's kingdom, power and glory are "for ever," you are recognizing the eternal nature of the One to whom you pray the Lord's Prayer.

When you acknowledge that God is "for ever," you are identifying your request with the eternal plan and purpose of God.

When you conclude your prayer with "for ever," you are asking God for permanent results from the Lord's Prayer.

AMEN

We experience many endings in life. We tell our friends "Good-bye" or "So long." Sometimes we say, "God bless you" or we just wave. Just as it is important how we leave people, so it is imperative how we "sign off" with God. Christians end their prayer saying "Amen," which means "so be it," or "so let it stand," or "my prayer stands before God on the basis of what it is...so be it."

When you end the Lord's Prayer, you tell God:

"I've prayed sincerely...so my prayer stands."

Or, "I've prayed according to Your pattern...so my prayer stands."

Or, "I've committed my answer to You...so my prayer stands."

Or, "I've prayed Your words, which is the best anyone can do...so my prayer stands."

Amen!!

KEEPING A PRAYER JOURNAL

If you have been keeping a journal since reading this book, you can review your spiritual journey of praying daily the Lord's Prayer. Go back and review the lessons you have learned and the answers to prayer you have received. Put into words these lessons and these answers to prayer.

This chapter discusses how to end praying the Lord's Prayer. Write out how you have been ending your daily prayer. Then, after reading this chapter, write how you intend to end your prayers.

1. What are the lessons you have learned by daily praying the Lord's Prayer?
2. How are you praying differently the Lord's Prayer?
3. What are some answers you have received since you have prayed daily the Lord's Prayer?
4. What has been your attitude as you have ended praying the Lord's Prayer?

5. What new things have you learned to "wrap up" your daily praying of the Lord's Prayer?

The following "prayer checklist" is another way to use your prayer journal.

PRAYER CHECKLIST			
For thine is the kingdom, the power, and the glory. Amen. *List how you have ended praying.*	**How are you doing?** **(check one)**		
	Lousy	*Average*	*Great*
1. Has God been given sovereign control?			
2. Do you recognize what God can do?			
3. Has God been given credit for answers to prayer?			
4. Do you have faith God will answer?			
5. Do you have greater hope after praying?			
6. Has God been praised through your prayers?			

THREE-STEP BIBLE STUDY

HOW TO END PRAYING THE LORD'S PRAYER

A regular feature in this book is the Three-Step Bible Study. In Step 1—Read the question and think through the answer you might write. Step 2 consists of reading and studying the printed Bible verse to discover how the Word of God answers the question. In Step 3—Write the answer in the space provided.

1. The conclusion of the Lord's Prayer has similar concluding requests of an Old Testament prayer. What are they?

> "Thine, O Lord, is the greatness, and the power, and the glory, and the victory, and the majesty: for all that is in the heaven and in the earth is thine; thine is the kingdom, O Lord, and thou art exalted as head above all."
> —1 Chronicles 29:11

_____
_____
_____
_____

2. What should be our attitude when we pray "Thine is the kingdom"?

> "But seek ye first the kingdom of God, and his righteousness; and all these things shall be added unto you."
> —Matthew 6:33

_____
_____
_____
_____

3. What should be our attitude when we pray "Thine is the power"?

> "And Jesus came and spake unto them, saying, All power is given unto me in heaven and in earth."
> —Matthew 28:18

_____
_____
_____
_____

4. Who should get credit for answers to our prayers and why should we give Him credit?

> "Now unto the King eternal, immortal, invisible, the only wise God, be honour and glory for ever and ever. Amen."
> —1 Timothy 1:17

_____

_____

_____

_____

5. How can the Lord's Prayer increase our faith to receive answers from God?

> "But without faith it is impossible to please him: for he that cometh to God must believe that he is, and that he is a rewarder of them that diligently seek him."
> —Hebrews 11:6

_____

_____

_____

_____

6. Abraham, a man of great faith, received answers from God because of his great hope in God. Describe this hope.

> "Therefore it is of faith, that it might be by grace; to the end the promise might be sure to all the seed;...which is of the faith of Abraham; who is the father of us all;...Who against hope believed in hope, that he might become the father of many nations, according to that which was spoken."—Romans 4:16,18

_____

_____

7. When we pray the Lord's Prayer, we attach ourselves
    to God's larger program. Describe this program.

> "That at the name of Jesus every knee should bow, of
> things in heaven, and things in earth, and things under
> the earth; and that every tongue should confess that
> Jesus Christ is Lord, to the glory of God the Father."
> —Philippians 2:10,11
> "The kingdoms of this world are become the kingdoms of
> our Lord, and of his Christ; and he shall reign for ever and
> ever."—Revelation 11:15

WHAT TO SAY
WHEN YOU HAVE
PRAYED IT ALL

Rightly praying the Lord's Prayer each day will guarantee that you say everything to God that you need to say, and that you say it in the right way. When you follow the sequence of petitions in the Lord's Prayer, you know you have approached God right because you are following His guidelines.

Just repetitiously using the Lord's Prayer, however, will not be effective unless you have the right attitude of heart. Jesus suggested that we must accompany this prayer with adoration and worship from the heart.

The Lord's Prayer is not an access code that automatically opens the door to a security area. Nor is it like a credit card that allows you to dial an 800 number to get what you want.

You cannot count on the Lord's Prayer to protect you as a vaccination would, nor is it like a country-club membership that gives you special privileges. You must believe that God exists and that God will reward those who "diligently seek him" (Heb. 11:6).

When you talk to God, pray the Lord's Prayer...with all your heart...with all your mind...with all your spirit...and with all your physical being.

Just as Jesus told us to love our neighbors as ourselves, so we must pray in concert with others in God's family. We must come with them

to God's throne, saying, "Our Father..." and "Give us...forgive us...
lead us...and deliver us."

ALWAYS PRAY

Prayer is something you must always do. So you must
always be *learning* to pray, you must always be *practicing*
prayer, and you must always be *living* prayer.
"Pray without ceasing."—1 Thessalonians 5:17

When you have finished praying the Lord's Prayer, you have said
everything to God you need to say, you know everything you need to
know and you have become everything God requires you to become.
We can pray no more except to conclude, "Thine is the kingdom, and
the power, and the glory, for ever. Amen!"

APPENDICES

APPENDIX A

ARGUMENTS FOR AND AGAINST RECITING THE LORD'S PRAYER

For centuries Christians have debated the merits of formally reciting the Lord's Prayer. As you can see from the following summaries of this discussion, there are good arguments on both sides of the issue.

WHY THE LORD'S PRAYER SHOULD NOT BE RECITED

1. There is no record of this prayer being repeated by the disciples or a New Testament church.
2. The instructions to the churches as recorded in the Epistles include no commands to recite the Lord's Prayer.
3. Jesus instructed His disciples, "When ye pray, use not vain repetitions" (Matt. 6:7).
4. The disciples asked Jesus, "Teach us to pray [verb]," (Luke 11:1). They did not ask, "Teach us a prayer [noun]." So He gave them the Lord's Prayer as a pattern, not something to recite.
5. The Lord's Prayer is recorded in Matthew (6:9-13) and Luke (11:2-4) at different times in Jesus' ministry using different wording. If He intended us to memorize and repeat it, He would have used the same words.

Conclusion: The Lord's Prayer is not a prayer just to be repeated, but a pattern to enable us to include everything we are required to pray when we talk to God.

WHY THE LORD'S PRAYER SHOULD BE RECITED

1. Because Jesus commanded, "When ye pray, say Our Father...."
2. Because it touches every kind of prayer, and thus helps develop a full prayer life.
3. Because it fulfills all our spiritual obligations to God.
4. Because it causes us to grow in every part of our spiritual life.
5. Because our memory is not perfect, and reciting the Lord's Prayer supplies important elements of prayer we might otherwise forget. When we overlook praying about any area of our Christian life, we hurt our spiritual growth.
6. Because of the example of godly Christians who have benefited from praying the Lord's Prayer through the ages.
7. Because the churches that first prayed this prayer were established by the apostles.
8. Because it has worked in the author's personal life.

WHY WE SHOULD PRAY THE LORD'S PRAYER BOTH PUBLICLY AND PRIVATELY

WHY THE PRAYER SHOULD BE PRAYED PUBLICLY

1. Because Jesus first instructed a group, not an individual, to pray the prayer: "When *ye* pray say, *Our* Father...."
2. Because it was a group of disciples who asked Him, "Teach *us* to pray."
3. Because Jesus used the plural pronouns "us," "our" and "we," suggesting He had in mind that more than one person would be praying the prayer.
4. Because there is no first person pronoun in the Lord's prayer.
5. Because congregations have prayed the Lord's Prayer publicly since the first century.
6. Because when a church prays the Lord's Prayer, a community of people are lifted together to God, as a corporate body.

WHY THE PRAYER SHOULD
BE PRAYED PRIVATELY

1. Although Jesus said to pray "Our Father" in response to a group request, and although He used plural pronouns, the prayer also meets the needs of the individual who needs a guide to praying. The prayer seems to be more than a prescription for corporate prayer at public meetings.

2. The reason Jesus did not use individual personal pronouns such as "I," "My" and "Me" is that these pronouns can develop selfish living and ego-driven prayers. Jesus used plural pronouns to develop humility in prayer; but we can pray the Lord's Prayer as individuals.

3. The Bible does not prohibit us from personally praying the Lord's Prayer.

4. Church history is filled with faithful, dedicated Christians who prayed the Lord's Prayer privately.

5. It is easier to apply the formula of the Lord's Prayer and to emphasize the various petitions of the Lord's Prayer when you are not following a group's lead, but praying privately.

6. The prayer is more personal when we recite it individually, avoiding the danger of the "vain repetitions" Jesus warned against.

7. No illustration is provided in the New Testament that the prayer was ever recited by a group.

⎯✑ APPENDIX C ✒⎯

CONTRAST BETWEEN MATTHEW'S AND LUKE'S ACCOUNTS OF THE LORD'S PRAYER

Although some authorities view Matthew 6 and Luke 11 as different versions of the same event, the following comparison supports the author's view that they are two different incidents.

MATTHEW 6	LUKE 11
1. Setting—given in the Sermon on the Mount	1. Setting—disciples ask Jesus to teach them to pray
2. Precontext—giving money ("alms")	2. Precontext—disciples see Jesus' model of prayer (v. 1)
3. Prayer as evidence of a humble spirit, versus pride	3. Prayer as a father-child relationship
4. Against public display	4. Example of private prayer
5. To Jews in danger of meaningless repetition	5. To Gentiles to teach the meaning of prayer
6. "After this manner"—a guide or model for private prayer	6. "When you pray, say"— exact wording and public repetition implied
7. "In earth as it is in heaven"	7. "As in heaven, so in earth"
8. Give us bread (aorist [instantly])	8. Give us bread (present [continually])
9. Give us bread today	9. Give us bread each day
10. Forgive us our debts	10. Forgive us our sins
11. As we forgive our debtors	11. We have already forgiven others
12. Thine is the kingdom... power...glory	12. Not in Luke's version

The Lord's Prayer Is...

Talking,
listening,
opening up,
loving,
meditating,
asking,
magnifying,
thinking,
changing,
waiting,
confessing,
worshiping,
exalting,
enjoying...
God.

Steps to Peace with God

 Step 1 God's Purpose:
Peace and Life

God loves you and wants you to experience peace and life—abundant and eternal.

The Bible Says . . .

". . . we have peace with God through our Lord Jesus Christ." **Romans 5:1**

"For God so loved the world that He gave His only begotten Son, that whoever believes in Him should not perish but have everlasting life." **John 3:16**

". . . I have come that they may have life, and that they may have it more abundantly." **John 10:10b**

Since God planned for us to have peace and the abundant life right now, why are most people not having this experience?

 Step 2 Our Problem:
Separation

God created us in His own image to have an abundant life. He did not make us as robots to automatically love and obey Him, but gave us a will and a freedom of choice.

We chose to disobey God and go our own willful way. We still make this choice today. This results in separation from God.

Our choice results in separation from God.

The Bible Says . . .

"For all have sinned and fall short of the glory of God." **Romans 3:23**

"For the wages of sin is death, but the gift of God is eternal life in Christ Jesus our Lord." **Romans 6:23**

People
(Sinful)

God
(Holy)

Our Attempts

There is only one remedy for this problem of separation.

Through the ages, individuals have tried in many ways to bridge this gap . . . without success . . .

The Bible Says . . .

"There is a way that seems right to man, but in the end it leads to death." Proverbs 14:12

"But your iniquities have separated you from God; and your sins have hidden His face from you, so that He will not hear." Isaiah 59:2

Step 3

God's Remedy: The Cross

Jesus Christ is the only answer to this problem. He died on the Cross and rose from the grave, paying the penalty for our sin and bridging the gap between God and people.

The Bible Says . . .

". . . God is on one side and all the people on the other side, and Christ Jesus, Himself man, is between them to bring them together . . ." 1 Timothy 2:5

"For Christ also has suffered once for sins, the just for the unjust, that He might bring us to God . . ." 1 Peter 3:18a

"But God demonstrates His own love for us in this: While we were still sinners, Christ died for us." Romans 5:8

God has provided the only way . . . we must make the choice . . .

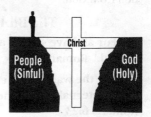

Step 4 Our Response: Receive Christ

We must trust Jesus Christ and receive Him by personal invitation.

The Bible Says . . .

"Behold, I stand at the door and knock. If anyone hears My voice and opens the door, I will come in to him and dine with him, and he with Me." Revelation 3:20

"But as many as received Him, to them He gave the right to become children of God, even to those who believe in His name." John 1:12

". . . if you confess with your mouth the Lord Jesus and believe in your heart that God has raised Him from the dead, you will be saved." Romans 10:9

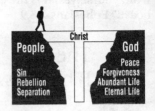

Is there any good reason why you cannot receive Jesus Christ right now?

How to receive Christ:

1. Admit your need (I am a sinner).
2. Be willing to turn from your sins (repent).
3. Believe that Jesus Christ died for you on the Cross and rose from the grave.
4. Through prayer, invite Jesus Christ to come in and control your life through the Holy Spirit. (Receive Him as Lord and Savior.)

What to Pray:

Dear Lord Jesus,

I know that I am a sinner and need Your forgiveness. I believe that You died for my sins. I want to turn from my sins. I now invite You to come into my heart and life. I want to trust and follow You as Lord and Savior.

In Jesus' name. Amen.

_____   _____
Date   Signature

God's Assurance:
His Word

If you prayed this prayer,

The Bible Says...

"For 'whoever calls upon the name of the Lord will be saved.'"
Romans 10:13

Did you sincerely ask Jesus Christ to come into your life? Where is He right now? What has He given you?

"For it is by grace you have been saved, through faith—and this is not from yourselves, it is the gift of God—not by works, so that no one can boast." Ephesians 2:8,9

The
Bible Says...

**"He who has the Son has life; he who does not have the Son of God does not have life. These things I have written to you who believe in the name of the Son of God, that you may know that you have eternal life, and that you may continue to believe in the name of the Son of God."
1 John 5:12–13, NKJV**

Receiving Christ, we are born into God's family through the supernatural work of the Holy Spirit who indwells every believer...this is called regeneration or the "new birth."

This is just the beginning of a wonderful new life in Christ. To deepen this relationship you should:

1. Read your Bible every day to know Christ better.
2. Talk to God in prayer every day.
3. Tell others about Christ.
4. Worship, fellowship, and serve with other Christians in a church where Christ is preached.
5. As Christ's representative in a needy world, demonstrate your new life by your love and concern for others.

God bless you as you do.

Billy Graham

If you want further help in the decision you have made, write to:
Billy Graham Evangelistic Association P.O. Box 779, Minneapolis, Minnesota 55440-0779